AF840642

Iain Dodd is a solicitor and a Partner at Fletchers Solicitors specialising in catastrophic injury claims arising from clinical negligence, where he also leads the brain injury unit. Iain has extensive experience of managing stroke (and other) claims of the upmost severity acting on behalf of claimants.

A Practical Guide to Stroke Claims in Clinical Negligence

A Practical Guide to Stroke Claims in Clinical Negligence

Iain Dodd
Solicitor and Partner
Fletchers Solicitors

Law Brief Publishing

Published 2025 by Law Brief Publishing, an imprint of Law Brief Publishing Ltd
30 The Parks
Minehead
Somerset
TA24 8BT

www.lawbriefpublishing.com

Paperback: 978-1-916698-87-1

FOREWORD

Clinical negligence claims have become an increasingly specialized area of litigation. Few would venture into the field without a sound understanding of the principles underpinning such claims.

In this excellent and clearly-written guide, Iain Dodd charts a course through the complexities associated with personal injury claims for stroke arising from medical mismanagement. He does so as an experienced and highly-respected practitioner in the clinical negligence field, with hands-on experience of navigating such claims to a successful conclusion. Beginning with an explanation of the medical terminology, the book goes on to set out in a clear and logical manner the steps required to investigate a potential stroke clinical negligence claim, including obtaining the right expert evidence, identifying potential breaches of duty, overcoming the difficulties in establishing causation, and quantifying the claim. Each chapter includes reference to the key principles, practical advice on managing the case and a helpful summary or checklist. In an area where it is all too easy for the inexperienced to be drawn down rabbit-holes, the need to focus on the real issues and to conduct cases proportionately are properly highlighted as recurring themes.

The text is clear and accessible throughout. Whilst Iain explicitly states in the Introduction that the book is not designed for experienced clinical negligence practitioners, I have no doubt that anyone embarking on the pursuit of a claim for damages arising from a stroke, from the relative novice to the seasoned specialist, will find this guide an indispensable tool.

David Knifton KC
Exchange Chambers

PREFACE

For practitioners involved in clinical negligence, it can sometimes be an uncomfortable topic of conversation if asked by someone you have met for the first time, "what job do you do?" I have always acted on behalf of claimants and when trying to explain my job and why I feel it so important, sadly, it can sometimes be met with raised eyebrows, a face of dismay and negative responses such as "how can you sue the NHS? They are amazing." This is one of the first accusatory responses to which, unfortunately, I have become accustomed. I retain sanguinity that other claimant practitioners have enjoyed a better experience in this regard.

In writing this book, I endeavour to avoid any criticism of the NHS and healthcare system within England and Wales. The work performed within the NHS is undoubtedly intensely challenging and relentless. This book is, in simple terms, a guide for those involved in clinical negligence arising from a stroke.

Returning to the conversation with my new acquaintance; once I have attempted (to the best of my ability) to expound that I represent people that have suffered catastrophic, life changing injuries, through no fault of their own, with the overarching goal to help them move forward with their life, a follow-up example occasionally develops.

"Actually, when I think about it, I know someone that had a stroke and they are only in their 20's. Do you think that could be because of medical negligence?" Many people will know of someone that has suffered from stroke. The thought of whether the stroke was avoidable because of clinical negligence is usually the last thing on a person's mind at the time. However, usually when some opportunity for reflection has passed, attention can be directed by the individual or their family to the question of why a stroke occurred.

I have endeavoured to correctly state the law as it is on 18th February 2025.

ACKNOWLEDGEMENTS

I would like to thank the following:

My clients, for whom it is my privilege to support them and their families to move forward following life-changing injuries.

My colleagues, as it is my pleasure to collaborate with them and share our passion for helping people.

The barristers, experts, and various professionals that I work with and instruct. I continue to learn so much from them.

Professor Pankaj Sharma, consultant neurologist, for proof reading Chapter One and recommending necessary adjustments.

David Knifton KC for his foreword and for being a magnificent silk.

Tim and Garry from Law brief publishing for providing the opportunity to prepare this book.

Finally, to Sarah, Sue and Pete for their unwavering encouragement and support.

Iain Dodd
18th February 2025

CONTENTS

INTRODUCTION

Overview

Stroke claims in clinical negligence can be particularly complex. It is usually a challenging issue to determine whether a stroke has arisen because of clinical negligence, or whether the outcome of a stroke would have been better with different/earlier treatment after the stroke has occurred. This book is aimed at legal practitioners, aspiring lawyers and others involved in clinical negligence claims arising from stroke. It takes the reader through practical issues and considerations in managing and progressing stroke claims. This is primarily achieved through the lens of a practitioner representing claimants, but principally, it is designed for any persons involved in stroke litigation.

This book is not a root and branch analysis or definitive guide of all issues relating to stroke litigation, and nor is it intended to endorse the pursuit of a clinical negligence claim. It is a text to share knowledge and information, and to enable people to enhance their understanding of how stroke cases might be handled by legal practitioners, by setting out common themes and issues. My vision is that practitioners can utilise this book to assist them in considering their cases.

Stroke prevalence

Strokes can be devastating and life changing; they can happen to anyone at any age. Alarmingly, stroke prevalence remains on the rise. The NHS Long Term Plan (2019) set outs the ambitions for the NHS over the next 10 years and identifies stroke as a clinical priority.

There has been a substantial increase, nationally and internationally, in the number of reported strokes in the last few decades. Worldwide, stroke is the second largest cause of death and around one third of stroke sufferers die due to stroke. The UK forecast is gloomy as stroke prevalence is expected to increase over the next decade, whereby in the year 2035, approximately 151,000 – 187,000 people annually in the UK are expected to be stroke survivors. This is an increase from approximately 100,000 – 136,000 annually at present. To put this in some context, in England alone, a stroke occurs every five minutes. There are estimated to be over 1.3 million stroke survivors in the UK. Stroke is a leading cause of adult disability and a common cause of dementia.

Sustaining a stroke can be cataclysmal to an individual, their family, friends, colleagues and others. As strokes are on the rise, the estimated cost for the NHS in managing strokes is expected to increase. It is clearly a clinical priority to reduce the number of strokes, to improve outcomes for stroke survivors and to assist with the cost of healthcare. The annual cost to the NHS of stroke is estimated to be in the billions and predicted to continue rising.

Clinical negligence litigation has a role to play; not in castigating professionals for alleged failures but to support identifying lessons to be learned. The mutual goal is improving healthcare in this field and reducing the number of adverse incidents and hopefully contributing to reducing overall stroke incidence.

Stroke claims

How stroke clinical negligence claims can be successfully pursued, or defended, will invariably fall to the individual facts, circumstances and issues that arise in each case. This book addresses practical issues in the context of a general guide. It does not distinguish the potential progress of claims subject to quantum value. Stroke cases from alleged clinical negligence fall into part of the unique categories of cases whereby they range from those that are likely to be modest in value – being less than £25,000; to catastrophic injury cases of multi-million-pound value with the claimant needing full-time professional care.

This book is not designed for experienced clinical negligence practitioners. Its purpose is to outline stroke cases in a legal context, as a readily accessible and straightforward narrative to be used by practitioners, law students, claimants, defendants, clinicians, expert witnesses, or those involved in clinical negligence litigation arising from stroke. It is to assist those with understanding the law further and common features in pursuing stroke claims. It is prepared on the basis of experience and knowledge. It is not to be regarded or intended as legal advice and it should not be treated as such.

Ethical dilemmas are not addressed and this book does not provide answers to stroke scenarios within clinical negligence. It is not designed to provide practitioners with the answers to winning a legal case arising from a stroke. It is a text, setting out the law as it is, in England and Wales in February 2025, with its core objective to be a resource tool when investigating and progressing legal claims arising from stroke. Whilst litigation is largely adversarial in nature, some steps are being taken in clinical negligence to reduce this more combative element towards a more collaborative approach; although much more is still to be done.

It should be recognised that most strokes do not occur as a result of clinical negligence. Even when legal cases are pursued, a high proportion of them will be unsuccessful. Cases will often fail to proceed, whether after receipt of the claimant's medical records, expert reports, pre-trial, or at trial. It is probable that only a minority of enquiries that are made to lawyers for stroke claims will ultimately be successful. Arguably, claimant lawyers are providing a useful resource for reducing the number of potential NHS complaints following stroke by screening out cases that lack sufficient prospects of success.

There are many challenges in successfully bringing a case arising from a stroke that should have allegedly been avoided due to substandard care, or for the treatment provided following stroke. In any clinical negligence matter, establishing breach of duty and causation can be difficult and complicated. Stroke cases can be especially arduous in proving either aspect. Experience alone suggests that failure to be able to establish causation in stroke cases is a common reason for cases being unable to get off the ground.

This book does not delve into the realms of pursuing claims when treatment was provided privately, as opposed to under the NHS. An entire topic could be dedicated to the issues that can arise when pursuing claims against private defendants. Generally, for stroke cases, the defendants are often GPs, Ambulance Services/Trusts and NHS hospitals. There are inevitably cases brought against private defendants in stroke claims and the same hurdles will arise as in other clinical negligence cases, such as identifying the correct defendant, and the defendant having adequate professional indemnity insurance cover or resources to satisfy any claim or judgment for damages secured against them. The law surrounding the insurance arrangements required for private medics and hospitals is not currently synonymous with that when pursuing a claim against the NHS. There are plentiful texts that provide information and guidance on matters such as retainers, client care, procedure, case management and the various stages of clinical negligence claims. An assumption is made in this text that a representative for a claimant will act on a conditional fee agreement basis.

Ultimately, most stroke cases will be determined on the basis of the factual issues, such as the condition of the claimant at certain times, the chronology of events, the available documents and scientific knowledge, the witness evidence, and the Part 35 expert evidence.

Stroke cases can be won or lost; they are often complex, time consuming and have a level of risk – for both claimants and defendants in the litigation. For practitioners representing claimants, successfully concluding stroke cases is professionally rewarding but conversely, there are numerous cases that are unsuccessful, despite significant time, costs and effort placed into progressing them.

The structure of this book

This book is split into nine chapters that charts preliminary points, the common general progression of stroke claims and issues to consider. There are, inevitably, some overlapping themes.

The focus of the first three chapters is designed to assist with understanding a stroke, the commonplace investigations that practitioners may need to perform, liability expert evidence and frequent themes in the progress of clinical negligence stroke cases.

The middle chapters, four to six, explore issues with liability and quantum of stroke claims. Breach of duty and causation are discussed, followed by condition, prognosis and quantum evidence being detailed.

The final three chapters lay out common aspects arising with quantum, rehabilitation, and lastly, settlement considerations in respect of stroke cases.

Collaborative spirit

Finally, the more that practitioners, claimants, defendants, clinicians, and those involved in clinical negligence claims arising from stroke can co-operate further and develop a more collaborative relationship, the better for all. Despite the ongoing rise of stroke prevalence, there is some optimism that with developing scientific progress and stronger collaboration between those involved in stroke and stroke prevention, improvements can be made to help curtail the increasing prevalence of stroke.

CHAPTER ONE

AN OVERVIEW OF STROKE

Purpose and core issues

This book focuses on strokes affecting the brain rather than the spine (although the principles are the same) which is outside the scope of this text. This chapter is designed to provide an understanding of stroke and to become accustomed to key points in order to get to grips with some of the issues which permeate stroke cases. An understanding of the disease is essential to the management of any clinical negligence claim and stroke is no exception. If lawyers and litigants do not adequately understand the pathophysiology and aetiology of a stroke, they are unlikely to be well equipped to build and drive forward an efficient and effective legal case. With a better understanding of stroke, it will assist those involved in stroke litigation with recognising whether the primary contention is likely to be:

- Failure to avoid the stroke occurring in the first place; or

- Failure to lessen the impact of a stroke; or

- That there is unlikely to be sufficient merits in pursuing the particular matter.

One of the core issues in any legal stroke case is determining whether the stroke itself would have likely been avoided with earlier or alternative treatment/management/preventative measures. This chapter summarises in simple terms:

- What is a stroke.

- How stroke may occur.

- Damage caused by stroke.
- How stroke may be treated.
- Risk factors for stroke.
- Clinicians involved in stroke medicine.

What is a stroke

In short, unsophisticated terms, a stroke occurs when a blood vessel carrying oxygen and nutrients to the brain is either blocked by a clot or bursts and when that occurs those supplied parts of the brain cannot receive the required blood and oxygen, so its corresponding brain cells die. In more clinical terms, stroke is a clinical syndrome of presumed vascular origin characterized by sudden signs of focal disturbance of cerebral function which lasts longer than 24 hours. The National Institute for Health and Care Excellence (commonly known as NICE) guidelines sets out the following helpful definitions (as at December 2023) online:

https://cks.nice.org.uk/topics/stroke-tia/background-information/definition/#:~:text=Stroke%20is%20a%20clinical%20syndrome,hours%20or%20leads%20to%20death.

There are two main types of stroke which are:

1. Ischaemic;
2. Haemorrhagic.

Another type of stroke is a Transient Ischaemic Attack (TIA), discussed later in this chapter. Approximately 80% of strokes are ischaemic and 20% are haemorrhagic. There are further sub-classifications of these two main types of stroke (and of others) which are beyond the scope of this book but include:

Ischaemic:	Cryptogenic, cardiogenic embolic, small penetrating artery thrombosis (lacunar stroke) and large artery thrombosis (atherosclerotic disease).
Haemorrhagic:	Intracerebral haemorrhage (around 15%) and subarachnoid haemorrhage (around 5%).
Venous:	Cerebral venous thrombosis (1% of stroke) predominantly affecting women caused by blockage of the venous rather than arterial system. Its causes and management are distinct from ischaemic or haemorrhagic stroke.

Ischaemic stroke

An ischaemic stroke is, in essence, a lack of oxygen or occlusion. It is caused by a blockage of a vessel leading to the loss of blood supply (also known as infarct). With insufficient oxygen reaching the brain it fails to receive the necessary nutrients it requires. It is an episode of neurological dysfunction caused by focal, cerebral, spinal, or retinal cell death due to infarction following vascular occlusion or stenosis. As there is insufficient blood reaching the brain, the brain cells begin to rapidly die.

To deconstruct this further:

- Ischaemia means blood flow and oxygen are reduced in part of the body.

- Occlusion means blockage, or obstruction, or closing of an opening.

- Infarction means death of tissue resulting from a failure of blood supply.

- Stenosis means abnormally narrow or restricted.

Haemorrhagic stroke

A haemorrhagic stroke is bleeding usually within the brain. It is rapidly developing neurological dysfunction due to a focal collection of blood from within the brain parenchyma or ventricular system, or bleeding into the subarachnoid space in the brain that is not caused by trauma. A haemorrhagic stroke occurs when blood vessels within the brain burst. The main risk factor for this type of stroke is age, while the commonest modifiable risk factor is hypertension.

To again deconstruct this:

- Haemorrhagic means bleeding; here, in the location of inside or around the brain.

- Subarachnoid space is the space between arachnoid matter and pia matter. It surrounds the brain and spinal cord and lies between the membranous layers.

For most people, the haemorrhage is caused by a cerebral (intracranial) aneurysm. Aneurysms develop at the site of a defect in the wall of the intracranial blood vessels. The weakened wall balloons out to form a blood-filled sac, known as a saccular aneurysm. This is unstable and may rupture causing haemorrhage into and around brain structures. In about 10% of people, the haemorrhage is caused by an arteriovenous malformation (AVM), a condition where blood vessels cluster together and form abnormal connections that are weak and prone to bleeding. In another 10% investigation reveals no evident vascular abnormality and the aetiology remains unknown. People that have suffered haemorrhagic stroke usually describe their worst ever headache (which is the result of red blood cell induced irritation of the tissues surrounding the brain), vomiting and collapsing, with loss of consciousness. The most characteristic feature is a sudden onset severe headache.

Throughout this book there are references to cited cases. A range of cases are selected which are intended to buttress the surrounding narrative. To begin with, a case relating to subarachnoid haemorrhage. In *Holt v Edge* [2007] EWCA Civ 602 a GP was not negligent for failing to diagnose a subarachnoid haemorrhage and refer the claimant to hospital sooner when the claimant had not presented with the usual symptoms. The claimant appealed the High Court judge's decision ([2006] EWHC 1932) dismissing her claim. Briefly, she had fallen in the shower, injuring herself. The emergency doctor visited later that evening and found the claimant had suffered a minor neck injury and advised her to see her GP in the morning. The GP visited the next day and confirmed the diagnosis. Two days later, the claimant attended hospital and was diagnosed as having suffered a subarachnoid haemorrhage. Following surgery undertaken three days later the claimant suffered a stroke. The defendant admitted breach of duty in failing to ensure the claimant was spoken to by a doctor earlier on the day of the accident but denied liability for her injuries. Her appeal was dismissed. It was held that the claimant had not presented with the usual symptoms of a subarachnoid haemorrhage (as described in the preceding paragraph) and the admitted breach made no difference to the eventual outcome of the surgery.

It was determined that if a telephone triage had been performed it would have made no difference because the defendant would not have learned anything to cause them to refer the claimant immediately to hospital. The key symptoms of a sudden pounding headache and vomiting had not been present when the initial call had been made to the surgery, or when the emergency doctor had visited in the evening. Although the defendant should have asked about vomiting, there was no evidence that if they had done so the claimant would have responded in a manner that would have required her to be immediately referred to hospital.

Transient Ischaemic Attack

A Transient Ischaemic Attack is usually known as a "TIA" or a mini-stroke. A TIA requires a person to make a full recovery within 24 hours. Otherwise, it is described as a minor stroke. Thus, a diagnosis of TIA cannot be possible until a person has been examined beyond the 24-hour period and shown to have made a full recovery. The majority of people with a TIA have a full resolution of symptoms within one hour. Those with residual deficits after one hour are more likely to continue to have some deficits the following day and thereafter. This would then be deemed a minor stroke.

Around 20% of people admitted to hospital with stroke show signs of progression within the first 24 hours. The mechanisms of progression are not well understood. One reason for deterioration is that the collateral blood flow supplying blood to an area of ischaemia fails so that area of ischaemia extends. Another reason is that toxic chemicals are released from ischaemic tissue extending the area of infarction beyond the initial core of the infarction. Another is that there is a spread of the thrombus responsible for the initial area of ischaemia from the initial site of occlusion to involve a greater extent of the artery occluding additional branches of the artery.

The incidence of TIAs in people between the ages of 15 and 44 years was one in 50,000 of the population per year. This was based on a study carried out by Dennis in 1989 in Oxfordshire. In relation to hemiplegic migraine based on a study from Denmark by Thomsen in 2002, sporadic hemiplegic migraine had an incidence of one in 250,000 per annum in the population under the age of 40 years. Lebedeva 2018 found that headache occurred in 30% of patients with TIA, but unilateral headache only occurred in 15%. A study by Coull in 2004 showed that 15% of strokes were preceded by a TIA.

A takeaway point from this is, even though a TIA may completely resolve within 24 hours, it is arguably important for clinicians to take the symptoms very seriously.

Symptoms of TIA are similar to stroke and can include:

- Visual disturbance. Generally, this can be caused either by TIA, or migraine. (Migraine is a severe usually throbbing headache associated with photo- and phono-phobia.) A TIA may block the ophthalmic artery causing visual disturbance only in that one eye, or if the clot is in the occipital lobe it could cause disturbances in both eyes. It would be typical of TIA in one ophthalmic artery for the symptoms to be unilateral to that supplied eyeball.

- Facial droop. This could occur as a result of TIA or migraine. Right facial droop would need a clot to be in a specific part of the left brain controlling the (contralateral) right side of the face if it were TIA.

- Speech. It would be relevant to distinguish between:

    - Dysarthria: which would be more characteristic of migraine or a TIA/stroke in the brainstem; that could be described as slurring or struggling to talk due to physical effects on the face; and

    - Dysphasia: which is more typical of TIA/stroke affecting a particular centre in the brain which would more likely cause confused speech or a primary language disorder.

In *Bell v Bedford Hospital NHS Trust* [2019] EWHC 2704 (QB) there was an alleged failure by clinicians to diagnose sequential TIAs and prevent the claimant suffering a major stroke leaving her disabled. Breach of duty and causation were denied. Although breach of duty was established, HHJ Taylor held that causation failed. The claimant was unable to establish their likely compliance with advice/treatment (had it been given), and the underlying cause of the stroke was unclear, so the effect of medication could not be proved. There were two potential primary causes of the stroke; atherosclerosis and dissection. The claimant was unable to prove on balance that atherosclerosis was the cause of stroke and that adherence to taking medication after having a diagnosis of TIA given would have prevented the stroke occurring. This case along with *Holt* demonstrates some of the challenges for a claimant to succeed in proving their case in stroke litigation. That breach of duty can be established, in full or in part, but causation fails as the stroke would not have been prevented.

Stroke diagnosis

In order to assist with diagnosing stroke, some matters that clinicians will consider include the following:

1. Is the process vascular or a stroke-like mimic;
2. If it is a vascular process, then what location in the central nervous system (CNS) is the abnormality and which blood vessels supply that territory;
3. What is the disease mechanism – is it ischaemic or haemorrhagic.

A clinical assessment is required for a diagnosis which should include:

- The presence of previous stroke and any TIAs.
- Activity at the onset of the stroke.
- The temporal course and progression of the focal symptoms and findings.
- Accompanying symptoms.

Young stroke

Approximately several hundred children are diagnosed with stroke each year in the UK. The causes of stroke in children are usually specific and commonly related to haematological disorders such as sickle cell disease. Large (atherosclerosis) and small vessel disease are common causes in people over age 50 but they are very uncommon in people under the age of 30 (according to Rothwell et al). The commonest cause of stroke in young people is cardiac embolism (embolism is the blockage of a blood vessel by a blood clot or piece of fatty material or other debris in the blood stream).

All humans have a hole in the heart during foetal development. That hole usually closes at birth (except in around 25% of people) meaning that an abnormal pathway exists between 'dirty' unoxygenated venous blood and 'clean' oxygenated arterial blood. A clot can therefore find its way between the venous and arterial system leading directly to the brain. This 'patent foramen ovale' (PFO) is a common cause of stroke in younger people.

An alternative common cause of younger people with stroke is a dissection of one of the four in the neck vessels feeding the brain (two front carotid and two rear vertebral arteries). The lining of these vessels can become separated (dissected) creating a false lumen which blood then traverses slowly enough to allow it to clot and then emboli. Even minor trauma may cause such a dissection.

FAST

The FAST campaign was launched in February 2009 by the Department of Health to raise awareness about the signs of stroke and to encourage people to call the emergency services immediately. FAST stands for:

F Facial weakness

- can the person smile;
- Has their mouth or eye drooped.

A Arm weakness

- Can the person raise both arms.

S Speech difficulties

- Can the person speak clearly;
- Can the person understand what you say to them.

T Time

- Time to call 999 immediately.

Just one of the F, A, S symptoms should trigger a person to call the emergency services. A person does not need to have all three of the face, arm, and speech symptoms to require an assessment for potential stroke diagnosis.

Mechanisms of stroke

A stroke occurs when the flow of blood to part of the brain is cut off or interrupted. This is described above in terms of an ischaemic or haemorrhagic stroke. When the flow of blood stops, or is interrupted, the brain cells begin to suffer necrosis and die. In an ischaemic event, the brain neuronal cells rapidly die at a rate of around two million each minute. When the cells die, a loss of neuronal function occurs.

The blood flow to the brain is managed by two internal carotids (these are major blood vessels) and two vertebral arteries (these run through the spinal column into the neck and into the brain). The middle cerebral artery (MCA) is a large artery that supplies a substantial portion of one half of the brain. The MCA is fed by the carotid artery in the neck. Any disruption of blood supply to this vascular system will result in neuronal death.

Strokes are nearly always of abrupt onset. They are an abrupt neurological outburst caused by impaired perfusion (the passage of fluid) through the blood vessels to the brain. There can be many causes of stroke such as:

- Thrombus
- Embolus
- Vessel disease
- Rupture of an aneurysm
- Arterial

Hypertension (outlined below as risk factors) may cause ischaemic stroke by two mechanisms. Either by small vessel atherosclerosis (which is narrowing of the tiny vessels in the structures of the brain) or by large artery atherosclerosis which usually develops over many years. Hypertension causes haemorrhagic stroke as the tiny vessels can rupture under the pressure of chronic excess force.

Risk factors for stroke

There are numerous risk factors for stroke and the risk of stroke increases with age. The risk factors are usually regarded as modifiable and non-modifiable. The common causes of stroke include:

Non-modifiable	*Modifiable*
Age	High blood pressure (hypertension)
Gender	Atrial fibrillation
Race / ethnicity	Excess alcohol / drugs
Genetics / family history	Obesity / physical inactivity
	Diabetes
	Smoking

Hypertension and atrial fibrillation (AF) are the two most important modifiable risk factors for stroke. Cases surrounding alleged failure to prevent stroke in individuals with these conditions can occur. There are available measures to help reduce the risk of stroke which are discussed in chapter four. Tools such as the $ABCD^2$ score are used to estimate the risk of stroke occurring after a suspected TIA.

Hypertension and atrial fibrillation

Hypertension

Hypertension is high blood pressure. This is usually deemed to be more than 140/90 mmHg. Blood pressure is the measure of the force of blood pushing against vessel walls. It is measured in millimetres of mercury (mmHg). The higher number is systolic pressure, which is the force at which the heart pumps blood around the body. The lower number is diastolic pressure, the resistance to the blood flow in the vessels. High blood pressure / hypertension is the biggest modifiable risk factor for stroke. Most cases of essential hypertension have no underlying cause identified. With secondary hypertension, a direct cause is ascertained such as use of steroid medications, kidney disease and endocrine disease. The treatment of hypertension can include antihypertensives such as drugs like beta blockers and ACE inhibitors. Lifestyle changes are also advised like weight loss and reducing alcohol, caffeine and salt levels. Untreated hypertension can lead to stroke, amongst other diseases.

Atrial fibrillation (AF)

This is the most common heart rhythm disturbance. It is an irregular and erratic (often fast) heart beat. It increases the chances of blood clots forming in the heart, and these clots can then travel in the blood stream to the brain and cause a stroke. The prevalence of AF is predicted to double within the next 25 years as the population ages. The main causes of AF are hypertension (as above), atherosclerotic heart disease, hyperthyroidism and other heart diseases. Some triggers of AF include alcohol / caffeine excess, smoking and recreational drugs. People will not always have symptoms but some symptoms include shortness of breath, tiredness, chest pain, palpitations and light-headedness.

AF results in a fivefold increase in the risk of stroke and doubles the risk of death. Around 20-25% of all strokes are caused by AF but for people over age 80, around 30-40% are AF induced. People with AF should usually have a personalised clinical assessment for their care to include stroke awareness and measures to help prevent stroke. The CHA_2DS_2-VASc score is a comprehensive assessment of stroke risk in patients with AF. People with one or more risk factors are considered for anticoagulation.

Damage caused by stroke

Damage from a stroke can range from very minor through to catastrophic and fatal. A basic overview of damage is set out below but of course, ordinarily, obtaining condition and prognosis expert evidence will be required to address the damage caused, as will be examined in chapters six and seven.

The National Institute of Health Stroke Scale (NIHSS) score is an international score to assess the functional ability of a person following stroke. It is a systematic, quantitative assessment tool to measure stroke-related neurological deficit. In clinical practice it can be used to evaluate and document the neurological status in acute stroke patients, determine appropriate treatment and assist in standardising communication between healthcare practitioners. It is a 15-item neurological examination stroke scale used to evaluate the effects on the levels of consciousness, language, neglect, visual-field loss, extraocular movement, motor strength, ataxia, dysarthria, and sensory loss. Ratings for each item are scored on a 3- to 5-point scale, with 0 being normal. Scores range from 0 to 42, with higher scores indicating greater severity. Stroke severity based on NIHSS scores are as follows:

0:	No stroke
1–4:	Minor stroke
5–15:	Moderate stroke
16–20:	Moderate/severe stroke
21–42:	Severe stroke

The modified Rankin Scale (mRS) is a functional assessment scale that measures the degree of disability or dependence of people who have suffered stroke. It is a 6 point disability scale with possible scores ranging from 0 to 5. A separate category of 6 is usually added for people who have died. The mRS is the most widely used outcome measure in stroke clinical trials. It is recommended at three months following hospital discharge. The scale runs from perfect health without symptoms to death, and is categorised as follows:

0: No symptoms.

1: No significant disability; able to carry out all usual activities, despite some symptoms.

2: Slight disability; able to look after own affairs without assistance, but unable to carry out all previous activities.

3: Moderate disability; needs some help, but able to walk unassisted.

4: Moderately severe disability; unable to attend to own bodily needs without assistance, and unable to walk unassisted.

5: Severe disability; needs constant nursing care and attention, bedridden, incontinent.

6: Death.

Other tools can be utilised to predict outcomes following stroke but they are not measures to the test the damage sustained. The DRAGON score is one of the scores used to predict a stroke outcome three months after an ischaemic stroke. The clinical features of the DRAGON score, which influence the outcome are:

- The appearance of the CT scan prior to thrombolysis.
- Dependency level of the person before thrombolysis using mRS.
- Age.
- Blood sugar level.
- Onset to treatment time.
- NIHSS on admission.

The above are summarised to provide an understanding of how clinicians will assess people in practice. As stated above, it will usually be necessary to obtain independent expert evidence on the clinical and functional damage sustained.

Imaging to identify stroke

A CT head scan is the most immediate scan performed following a suspected stroke. CT scans are good at showing blood. It will usually always be performed before a MRI scan is considered. A CT head scan is used to exclude haemorrhagic stroke, or some stroke mimics. A normal scan does not exclude an ischaemic stroke. A CT scan appearance to indicate stroke normally takes several hours to show on the scan. A 'normal' CT scan is often reported but does not exclude a hyper acute (very recent) stroke.

MRI scanning can be performed which can assist to determine the cause of the stroke. Performing this scan would not usually occur before considering whether to offer thrombolysis (summarised below). The location of an infarction on the MRI scan can be indicative of how it originated. For example, with a history of progressive stroke and hypertension, this is typical of anterior choroidal infarction. MRI scan does not usually add much to the immediate treatment plan if performed immediately following stroke, except potentially in cases of 'wake up' stroke when the timing of the stroke and likelihood of clot busting drugs being successful can be better judged.

Treatment of stroke

Treatment to help prevent stroke includes medication to prevent and dissolve blood clots, reduce blood pressure and cholesterol levels. Treatment following stroke depends on the type of stroke suffered. Surgery may be required as a preventative measure or following stroke.

Embolization procedures may be required. The most common treatments are outlined below.

Chemical treatment

There are two main chemical treatments of acute stroke. These are:

1. Thrombolysis: this treatment chemically breaks up a blood clot so as to reconstitute normal blood flow back to brain tissues.

2. Antiplatelets and anticoagulants: usually aspirin and warfarin (or NOAC which is Non-vitamin K Antagonist Oral Anticoagulant). Sometimes heparin is given. Aspirin does not break up a blood clot. Its effect (if it works) is to stop a blood clot enlarging and reduces the tendency of a clot to break up and send part of the clot migrating further along the circulatory system, thereby potentially causing serious harm. Warfarin/NOAC (and heparin) is an anticoagulant. It works by interfering with the clotting mechanism in such a way that the clot stops growing and spreading. Warfarin is usually the treatment of choice for people with atrial fibrillation.

1. Thrombolysis

Thrombolysis is a well-established treatment for acute ischaemic stroke and its primary purpose is to act as a powerful blood thinner. Thrombolysis is a clot busting drug. The name of the drug is Alteplase but is also referred to as "rt-PA" (recombinant tissue plasminogen activator). It is sometimes described as a "clot buster" as it works by dissolving the clot. For this process to be effective, there must be recanalization of the artery and then the effect relates to how much of the brain remains salvageable following restoration of blood flow. However, post-surgery, administrating this type of medication could itself be potentially life-threatening so thrombolysis is contraindicated following surgery.

Thrombolysis can usually only be given within 4.5 hours of the onset of symptoms. The sooner the treatment is given, the higher likelihood of a better outcome. The phrase "time is brain" is often used. It is the best available treatment for an acute stroke according to national guidelines. The "door to needle" time to give thrombolysis treatment is subject of national audit and monitoring in the Sentinel Stroke National Audit Programme (SSNAP). This is the most comprehensive source of data to improve the quality of stroke care in England, Wales and Northern Ireland.

The National Clinical Guideline for Stroke from the Royal College of Physicians recommends that thrombolysis can be administered at up to 4.5 hours of known onset (of neurological symptoms) provided the person meets certain strict clinical criteria. It is particularly important that the onset time is clear with a high degree of certainty as thrombolysis has potentially serious and harmful side effects if not administered correctly and in an approved timely manner.

A person should not receive thrombolysis before a CT scan because a stroke can be caused by intracerebral haemorrhage which can only be shown on CT or MRI brain scan. Thrombolysis in the presence of cerebral haemorrhage is dangerous and may be catastrophic.

2. *Antiplatelets and anticoagulants*

Aspirin

This was the first effective antiplatelet drug used widely. It is used to make blood less sticky and help prevent blood from developing a potentially dangerous clot. Its prescription, or lack of, can be a common feature in stroke litigation and this is revealed further in chapters four and five.

Clopidogrel

This antiplatelet medicine helps prevent platelets from sticking together and forming a blood clot. It is often prescribed to people at risk of stroke or following stroke and it will be a common medication to see if acting in numerous stroke claims. It can be prescribed with or instead of low-dose aspirin.

Heparin

Heparin is an anticoagulant and works by bathing the thrombus. It does not dissolve the thrombus but it prevents propagation and enables the body's own mechanisms to recanalize the affected veins. In *Pickering v Cambridge University Hospitals NHS Foundation Trust* [2022] EWHC 1171 (QB) the claimant had a history of atrial fibrillation and had regularly been taking aspirin. She attended A&E with symptoms of pain, numbness, coldness and pallor (paleness of skin) in one leg. The A&E clinician diagnosed a resolved ischaemic event in her right leg and discharged her home with advice to recommence aspirin and follow up with her GP over the next five to seven days. Unfortunately for the claimant, she suffered a significant stroke at home three days later causing extensive disabilities.

The claimant alleged there was a failure by the A&E clinician in that she had likely suffered an embolus in her leg and to immediately administer heparin to prevent further embolism. Breach of duty was admitted during the trial (following cross-examination of the defendant's A&E expert), whilst causation remained denied. By the end of the trial there was one issue to determine which was whether, but for the defendant's negligence, the claimant would have avoided the stroke due to the beneficial effects of heparin treatment which should have been given and continued until she was provided with anti-coagulation. Ritchie J held that causation was established. If heparin had been administered on a timely basis, the secondary clot formation would have been prevented. This case is discussed again later in this book.

Warfarin

Warfarin is the most widely used anticoagulant in the UK. It enables blood to flow through veins more easily and making the blood less likely to clot. It is used to help reduce the risk of stroke and is shown to be effective at doing so for people with atrial fibrillation. It helps to prevent new blood clots from forming but it does not dissolve blood clots. Warfarin is explored further in chapter five.

Other anticoagulant medications (NOAC) include:

- Apixaban
- Dabigatran
- Edoxaban
- Rivaroxaban

These drugs (above) are increasingly replacing warfarin as they (reportedly) benefit from fewer side effects and may be easier for clinicians and patients to manage, dispensing with the need for regular blood tests.

There are other groups of medicines that are prescribed to assist in reducing the risk of stroke and to help prevent vascular disease such as statins. These medications can help lower the level of cholesterol in the blood. High cholesterol is potentially dangerous as it can lead to atherosclerosis and cardiovascular disease. Statins include:

- Atorvastatin
- Fluvastatin
- Pravastatin

- Rosuvastatin
- Simvastatin

Other medications

If a person suffers seizures following stroke, they usually require anti-epileptic medication such as Tegretol (carbamazepine). The use of this drug can have side-effects including leucopoenia (low white cells), thrombocytopenia (low platelets), movement disorders, vision disorders, vomiting and dizziness and headaches. There are numerous drug interactions with Tegretol which could limit the types of medication for unrelated issues.

Understanding the common medications involved in stroke prevention can help practitioners to identify issues more expeditiously.

Surgery

Sometimes surgery is required as treatment to help prevent stroke or following stroke. Some of the most common surgical procedures in relation to prevention of stroke or following stroke are:

Carotid endarterectomy

A carotid endarterectomy may be performed to help prevent stroke by removing the collection of fatty deposits (plaque) which can cause narrowing of the carotid artery and lead to stroke. It might be undertaken following stroke if it was caused by a blockage in a carotid artery in the neck. The aim is usually to remove the build-up of plaque.

Thrombectomy

Following stroke, a thrombectomy may be necessary in some instances. This is a surgical procedure to physically remove a blood clot and drain fluid from the brain. The aim of this surgery is to restore blood flow to the brain. Mechanical thrombectomy is only used for proximal intracranial large vessel occlusive stroke of the internal carotid, middle cerebral artery and basilar artery. Thrombectomy is not always indicated. Trials are ongoing to assess the efficacy of thrombectomy in occlusion sites other than the aforementioned.

Repair of aneurysm

Surgery is the main potential treatment following a haemorrhagic stroke. If a subarachnoid haemorrhage has occurred, then surgery to try and repair the burst blood vessel might be undertaken. Surgery to reduce pressure caused by a buildup of fluid can also be performed. The main two techniques for repair are coiling and clipping. Coiling is when the aneurysm is sealed off from the main artery to prevent it growing or rupturing again. Clipping is placing a metal clip around the base of the aneurysm to seal it shut.

<u>Clinicians often involved in stroke medicine</u>

Neurologist or stroke physician

The primary clinician to treat and manage stroke is a neurologist or stroke physician. The role of a neurologist in an acute setting post-stroke includes:

- Reviewing CT/MRI imaging;
- Assesses a person promptly;

- Makes a diagnosis;
- Treats, or refers for treatment.

A neurologist or stroke physician does not perform surgery. A neurologist treats diseases and disorders of the nervous system which includes the brain, spinal cord and nerves throughout the body. A stroke physician will usually treat people following stroke but they can treat those suspected of risk of stroke if a referral is made and accepted. These specialist disciplines are studied in chapter three.

Radiologist

The radiologist or neuroradiologist will review the imaging (CT / MRI for example) and report on that imaging. This will assist the neurologist / stroke physician to form a diagnosis. An interventional radiologist is a certain type of radiologist who undertakes procedures such as clipping of aneurysms or mechanical thrombectomies.

Neurosurgeon

If surgery is required following stroke, a neurosurgeon may perform the procedure.

Rehabilitation medicine

Following stroke, a rehabilitation medicine physician may become involved in leading the recommendations for management and rehabilitation of the person. This physician will provide interventions to people with disabling / complex conditions to try and optimise their recovery and functionality. They will commonly intervene when people have suffered stroke and other serious injuries. They can offer opinion on a person's capacity.

GP

The GP will often be the primary point of contact for stroke prevention. Other clinicians will of course be involved depending on the individual and their medical conditions. These are covered broadly in chapters three and four when outlining expert evidence and breach of duty issues for consideration.

Takeaway points

Within any successful claim or defence in clinical negligence, there needs to be an understanding of the medicine or science in that field. This is particularly true for stroke. Practitioners benefit from increasing their knowledge of medicine and it is not usually sufficient to simply try and rely upon experts. This chapter was not a detailed analysis of stroke, and how it originates, as the author is not qualified in medicine. However, a baseline understanding of stroke assists in developing a potential legal case. A summary of this chapter is as follows:

- A stroke is the outcome of a blocked or burst blood vessel that results in that area of the brain failing to receive oxygen and nutrients that are necessary for its function, so the brain cells die.

- The two main types of stroke are:

    1. Ischaemic/TIA (most common); and

    2. Haemorrhagic (less common).

- If stroke is suspected, time is of the essence to seek urgent medical treatment. Think FAST. Time is brain.

- A CT head scan is the foremost route to diagnosis of stroke.

- Broadly, strokes can be fatal, very disabling, disabling, moderate, mild and minimal. The modified Rankin Scale (mRS) and National Institute of Health Stroke Scale (NIHSS) score are commonly used by clinicians to assess the outcomes following stroke.

- Antiplatelets and anticoagulants are prescribed to help prevent stroke occurring or following stroke.

- Thrombolysis is the main potential immediate treatment given following an ischaemic stroke.

- Thrombolysis usually has a maximum 4.5 hour time window to be administered from the onset of stroke.

- Surgery is the main potential treatment following a haemorrhagic stroke.

- Neurologists/stroke physicians are the primary physicians/clinicians that manage/treat people following stroke (or are suspected of stroke risk).

- Rehabilitation medicine physicians will likely be the lead clinician regarding any rehabilitation and disability management needs following a disabling stroke.

- In simple terms, consider as a core point from the outset of a claim, that liability in stroke clinical negligence cases will usually centre around:

    - Whether with adequate management the stroke would have likely been avoided altogether; or

- Whether a non-negligent stroke should have been treated differently and if so, whether that would have resulted in a better outcome.

CHAPTER TWO

INVESTIGATIONS INTO A POTENTIAL STROKE CLAIM

This chapter sets out the blueprint of the preliminary investigations commonly performed in stroke clinical negligence claims. The focus is on the common components of medical records and documents that are frequently of relevance in stroke cases. It seeks to capsulize the various factors to consider when reviewing medical records, guidelines regarding stroke, and general practical points.

Beginning the investigations

At a clinical negligence trial, a judge will often analyse the evidence, then make findings of fact, before moving on to set out how these interplay with the expert evidence and other issues. Thereafter, confirming their conclusions and deciding the case. Putting that in this context, a starting point will ordinarily be to obtain documents and then endeavouring to drill down the fact-finding exercises, beginning with:

- Obtaining the claimant's medical records.

- Obtaining any documentary evidence such as guidelines and policies.

- Pending the circumstances and preferences of matters, to simultaneously or sequentially, obtain preliminary lay witness evidence.

Once a valid retainer is in place, obtaining the medical records of the injured claimant will be the main first step. Like other clinical negligence cases, the importance of medical records in stroke claims cannot be underestimated. These records will provide significant insight. If additional medical records are located/obtained at a later date (it is not unsurprising for medical records to have parts of them missing during the initial requests) after preliminary investigations have been made, the course of a case can pivot. It is prudent to obtain them all, where possible, from the outset. Nevertheless, there will undoubtedly be times where practitioners reasonably determine that some medical records are not required to provisionally assess the prospects of success in a case and/or where proportionality plays a part.

Investigations should strive to establish as precisely as possible the circumstances leading up to and surrounding the stroke. The investigations will provide materials relevant to a claim but they can take a considerable amount of time to perform. They can sometimes reveal that other defendants (and occasionally a more favourable case to a claimant) are discovered upon an attentive review of the medical records. Therefore, records should be assessed with an open mind and flexibility to consider whom are the potential defendants and (again) whether the stroke itself would likely have been avoided, even if the claimant's initial concern is the immediate response to the treatment of their stroke.

The accuracy of medical records

Whilst a trial judge may accept that clinical records can be incomplete, terse, and inaccurate, the records are generally regarded as contemporaneous and made under a professional duty. In *Parsons v Isle of Wight NHS Trust* [2023] EWHC 3115 (KB) Ritchie J said in dicta:

> "*where there are medical notes made by professionals acting under professional duties to make proper notes, those notes carry weight.*"

Similarly, in *Synclair v East Lancashire Hospitals NHS Trust* [2015] EWCA CA 1283 Tomlinson LJ accepted that clinical records were "*inherently likely to be accurate.*" Nevertheless, in *Synclair*, the Court of

Appeal endorsed the trial judge's finding that the ward round medical record was in fact, inaccurate. See also a more extreme example of inaccurate records in the claimant's successful case of *Astley v Lancashire Teaching Hospitals NHS Foundation Trust* [2023] EWHC 1921 KB where Spencer J found (in a birth injury claim) that part of the midwifery notes were "*fabricated*" and "*inaccurate*". Therefore, consider with the claimant the accuracy of key medical records and analyse any challenges purported to them. For example:

- Do the records match the description the claimant and any other persons provided about their symptoms with what they say they told clinicians.

- Is the claimant able to evidence any challenge to the records if they allege inaccuracies.

- Are the records from the GP consistent with hospital/other records for events/attendances occurring in close proximity.

- Are there any aspects of the records considered to be omitted or missing such as neurological examinations, referral letters, telephone notes and so on.

In relation to seeking supporting evidence if investigating a challenge to the accuracy of medical records, the witness evidence will be important but also consider documentary evidence. This can include, for example, mobile phone communications whereby the claimant or family/friend has sent text/WhatsApp messages. This can reveal things such as the time of the message and highlights issues such as what the claimant said they told the clinician. Mobile phone (or email) communications can be revealing in stroke claims as the claimant may have messaged someone following a clinical appointment which illuminates that they mentioned specific symptoms. For example, blurred vision, or neurological weaknesses but this is not recorded in the medical records.

GP records

GP records should, ordinarily, set out the medical chronology to the claimant's birth, or first visit to a medical professional on the NHS. Claimants that have lived outside of the UK will usually only have their medical records available since living in the UK. Therefore, consider if any records from outside the UK need to be obtained. This can also include/apply to any clinical attendances during trips abroad/holidays if they might be relevant. GP records can provide a helpful overview and insight into a claimant's pre-existing and current medical issues. Even when a claimant has not visited their GP for some time preceding the stroke, reviewing the GP records can be useful.

When a claimant attends a hospital/clinic, the GP will often be the main or carbon copied correspondent to communications. There can be scenarios when correspondence from a hospital/clinic is purportedly not received by the GP, or vice versa. For example, if there is a telephone entry in the GP records calling a hospital discussing the claimant but no record of this appears in the hospital notes. Alternatively, a referral letter being visible in the GP notes but not contained in the hospital notes and it being alleged that it was never sent/received. Sometimes an inspection of the original medical records could be required. This will be uncommon but can occur if there is a dispute on correspondence ever being delivered/received. Investigations as to the method of referral letters being sent (emailed / posted / faxed) may be required to ascertain matters further. It is also worthwhile considering whether a clinician is likely to be a witness of fact.

When reviewing GP records in stroke cases, analyse matters that occurred before the stroke such as:

- The claimant's medications – for example, were they using antiplatelets/anticoagulants.

- If relevant, any blood pressure readings – for example, to consider hypertension.

- Any references to TIAs or mini strokes – to consider any actions after these events and making a list of the dates.

- References to migraine, headache, loss of vision/eye disturbance – for example, to consider any 'red flags' for stroke.

- Vomiting, dizziness, change/loss of consciousness.

- Facial numbness/weakness.

- Similarly, any references to neurological symptoms such as limb weakness / difficulty walking.

- Referrals (letters / emails / telephone calls etc.) and cross-referencing what occurred thereafter.

- Any follow-up appointments that could be of relevance such as to neurology, cardiology or vascular departments.

GP records can be informative and illuminating. Practitioners may recognise possible red flags for stroke in the history. Carefully reviewing them will be a useful exercise that assists in investigating matters.

Hospital records

In every stroke case the hospital records should be reviewed. When scrutinising these records to evaluate matters following a seemingly non-negligent stroke (usually for assessing thrombolysis/thrombectomy cases), some features to consider include:

- What was the claimant's arrival time at hospital.

- Who reviewed the claimant.

- What was the triage time.
- What was the CT scan time.
- What were any review time(s) by clinicians.
- What was the time of stroke diagnosis (if given).

The above considerations are based on stroke occurring when a person is not already in hospital and the preliminary investigations are on whether a non-negligent stroke was dealt with appropriately. However, hospital records should be analysed to consider any earlier attendances at hospital/clinics, along with correspondence, test results and so on that could have been indicative of potential warning signs of stroke occurring. Assess whether there is any potential lack of/inadequate treatment and other avenues that have led to a stroke that should have been avoided.

As with GP records, consider possible red flags for stroke (which are discussed throughout this book through the medium of cited cases and general commentary). There will be times when there were no indicators in the hospital records for stroke being a risk (or it being a risk that was unavoidable) but this should not deter investigations being performed in this regard.

Contemporaneous and historical clinical attendances can both be significant. In *Lyndon v Royal Free Hampstead NHS Trust* [2011] EWHC 2904 (QB) the claimant established that her stroke had been caused by a negligent failure, some 14 years earlier, to diagnose rheumatic fever and prescribe a continuing course of penicillin. When she was age 15, the claimant had been examined by a paediatrician, who negligently failed to take steps that would have resulted in a diagnosis of rheumatic fever and the consequent commencement of a 10-day course of treatment with penicillin, followed by penicillin prophylaxis for 10 years. The rheumatic fever had arisen from a Group A streptococcal throat infection. The penicillin prophylaxis would have prevented such further infections and attacks of rheumatic fever and the consequent damage to her heart. The claimant ultimately suffered a stroke caused by infective endocarditis.

Sweeney J held that the carditis from which the claimant suffered 14 years prior to stroke had been mild and transient and had not resulted in any permanent damage to her heart. Statistics were analysed indicating it was more than likely the claimant had not suffered permanent damage to her heart from the initial episode and that the stroke would have been avoided.

Ambulance records

If a claimant or someone on their behalf has dialled 999 (or 111) complaining of stroke-like symptoms, then these records, including any call recordings will be inciteful. For stroke cases where the onset of symptoms and timeframe to/at hospital is an issue, the ambulance records may set out potential factual details that feed into the relevant chronology. The word "potential" is used here to recount that the medical records may not always be accurate/correct so scrutinise them. When reviewing ambulance records, some pertinent things to consider sometimes includes:

- The time the call to the emergency services was made.
- The time the claimant, or the caller, gives as the start time of the claimant's onset of symptoms.
- Whether the claimant woke up (from sleeping) with symptoms (often known as a wake-up stroke).
- The symptoms described during the call and during the paramedic assessment.
- The priority level given by the dispatcher.

- The ambulance dispatch time.
- The arrival time of the ambulance at the claimant's location.
- Whether paramedics considered stroke as a potential diagnosis.
- Whether paramedics recorded symptoms consistent with stroke but did not consider stroke as a potential diagnosis.
- The distance from the claimant's location to hospital.
- The time it took from arrival, suspected diagnosis, to arrival in hospital.
- What, if any, call was made from paramedics to warn A&E of the claimant's arrival.
- What, if any, handover discussion was undertaken by paramedics and the hospital clinicians.

Ambulance records can sometimes help to try and verify the chronological timeline and the claimant's condition, particularly if a call recording and accurate call log is made. A copy of the call recording should be sought along with the transcription. Sometimes a transcript of the call is unavailable but if the recording is provided, it will help for it to be transcribed. Like GP/hospital records, historical input from the Ambulance Services prior to stroke may provide information that develops investigations further. For example, the Ambulance Services may have reviewed a claimant days/weeks/months/years prior to stroke and potentially not recognised symptoms that should have necessitated onward referral.

Paginated medical records

Most practitioners will obtain a form of paginated medical records. Elevating this where proportionate to do so would be to then prepare a focussed chronology of the paginated records deemed most crucial to the case once a first review of the records has been undertaken. Rigorously analysing the relevant medical records is needed to evaluate matters and as in other cases, make requests where records are deemed missing or incomplete.

Clinical Handbooks

The various Oxford Handbooks and other similar texts are often a helpful resource to review to cross reference medical/clinical guidelines and practice with the events in question. There is a Stroke Medicine Oxford Handbook available. Courts frequently reference Handbooks when delivering judgments in clinical negligence trials arising from stroke. Examples include:

- Neurology (Stroke Medicine);
- General Practice; and
- Clinical Haematology.

Locating relevant extracts from Handbooks that potentially apply to the facts of the claimant's case can assist in the investigations and assessing prospects of success. For example, in *Crammond v Medway NHS Foundation Trust* [2015] EWHC 3540 (QB) His Honour Judge Brian C Forster QC sitting as a Deputy High Court Judge stated:

> *"I have considered the extracts from the Oxford Handbook of Emergency Medicine and those from Emergency Medicine (Brown & Cadogan)."*

In this case, the claimant succeeded in establishing negligence arising from an ischaemic stroke secondary to acute coronary syndrome (ACS). There was an alleged failure to act appropriately on reported symptoms or to illicit a full history and failure to triage or stream the claimant to the treatment centre, rather than A&E. It was demonstrated that eliciting a history would have led to their admission and appropriate treatment to avoid the stroke.

Similarly, in *McCabe v Moore & Ors* [2015] EWHC 260 (QB) when delivering judgment for the claimant, Sir Robert Nelson made references to the Oxford Handbook of General Practice. In this case it was accepted by the GP experts that the Oxford Handbook sets out what a GP should understand. The claimant had suffered a stroke secondary to infective endocarditis. There was an alleged failure by the claimant's GPs to suspect infective endocarditis and refer the claimant to hospital. Breach of duty and causation were denied. The claim was successful against one of three GP defendants on breach of duty and causation. It was held that the third defendant failed to appreciate the significance of what the claimant had told them and it raised a "*red flag... and required elaboration... and that elaboration should have resulted in admission to hospital.*"

The claim prevailed on causation because the judge was satisfied that had the claimant been admitted to hospital, cardiology investigations would have started, resulting in antibiotics commencing which "*would have been sufficient to halt the infective process...* and... *have prevented the stroke.*" The other two claims were dismissed. This serves as an illustration of the potential importance of Handbooks (and red flags) for what a reasonable clinician should understand and therefore, researching the Handbooks can be highly informative. *McCabe* is revisited in chapter nine on the issue of settlement as the defendants obtained surveillance evidence on the claimant.

Policies and protocols

The proposed defendant may have in place relevant policies/protocols applicable to the incident or issues at hand. The majority of NHS Trusts have policies available for the management of a catalogue of conditions. It is important to analyse whether the defendant adhered to its own policy/protocols. Many of the policies are available publicly online but if not, a copy of the policy in place at the time of events should be requested from the Trust(s).

When considering the Trust's own policies, keep in mind that they may be outdated or deficient. If a Trust has complied with its own policies, this does not necessarily mean that they have a defence. In *Owers & Anor v Medway NHS Foundation Trust & Anor* [2015] EWHC 2363 (QB) (discussed below within the "Guidelines" sub-section) the Trust's own stroke pathway was deficient and breach of duty was partially admitted.

However, in *Marion O'Brien (Administratix of the estate of Mr John Berry (deceased)) v Guy's & St Thomas' NHS Trust* [2022] EWHC 2735 (KB) His Honour Judge Tindal held that the Trust complied with their own in-house policy guidelines and not the national guidelines; and the Trust (the doctor following the in-house guidelines) were not in breach of duty for departing from the national guidelines. The judge said:

> "*what is the relevance of (non) compliance with clinical guidelines (both national and 'in-house') to Bolam-negligence? However, the question has only been addressed relatively briefly in a few authorities I discussed with Counsel, possibly more rarely than one might expect given the prevalence of clinical guidelines… Guidelines are not a substitute for expert medical evidence on liability in that particular case and so will rarely – if ever – be wholly determinative.*"

Notwithstanding this, in-house guidelines are not of the same status as national guidelines and cannot be used to demonstrate that specific conduct is acceptable practice.

Guidelines

When investigating a stroke claim, research whether national or local guidelines are available in respect of the issues. For example, the National Clinical Guidelines for Stroke: https://www.strokeguideline.org/. These guidelines set out, amongst other things, recommendations for management of ischaemic stroke. This confirms that thrombolysis should be considered where treatment can be given within 4.5 hours. For people ineligible for thrombolysis who present with acute ischaemic stroke and have had the CT scan, the recommendation is aspirin to be given as soon as possible and within 24 hours.

The National Stroke Service Model dated May 2021: stroke-service-model-may-2021.pdf (england.nhs.uk) is another example that sets out what is understood to be best practice for the NHS in caring for adult (over 16 years of age) stroke patients. A highlight from this includes that systems should achieve a 90th centile call to needle time of 180 minutes for thrombolysis.

NICE guidelines may be applicable to the circumstances and indicate evidence of potential failures. If the claimant had a previous TIA, the December 2023 guidelines for suspected TIA might be a point to carefully review. See: https://cks.nice.org.uk/topics/stroke-tia/management/suspected-transient-ischaemic-attack/. In a similar vein, the NICE guidelines 2019 (updated in 2023) set out diagnosis and management of hypertension in adults which could be relevant if investigating a matter where the claimant had hypertension prior to stroke. See: https://www.nice.org.uk/guidance/ng136.

Various (Royal) College guidelines may be available and assist investigations. For example, the Royal College of Paediatrics and Child Health (RCPCH) Stroke Guidelines states aspirin should be initiated promptly after the diagnosis of arterial ischaemic stroke unless contraindicated. Or, away from paediatrics, if a matter relates to investigating input by an Optometrist for alleged delay or failure to refer following loss of vision followed by a later stroke, the College of Optometrists provides an "urgency of referrals" table. See:

Annex 4 Urgency of referrals table – College of Optometrists (college-optometrists.org)

Guidelines can be an important resource for breach of duty investigations and like Handbooks, judges may utilise them when assessing stroke claims. For example, in *Owers & Anor v Medway* (mentioned above) Mr Justice Stewart stated:

> *"I attach to this judgment... material sections of NICE clinical guidelines: Stroke, Diagnosis and initial management of acute stroke and transient ischaemic attack (TIA)."*

This case was a Fatal Accidents Act claim arising from stroke. There were alleged failures to diagnose and treat stroke either by way of thrombolysis or, if not a candidate for thrombolysis, by aspirin. Whilst breach of duty was partially admitted for failing to prescribe the deceased aspirin after the stroke, causation was denied. It was held that causation was not established as that breach had not caused or materially contributed to the adverse outcome.

Complaints and further information requests

A complaint may have been submitted prior to legal input, or made after lawyers are instructed. An admission within complaint correspondence is not a prima facie case of negligence but can assist to demonstrate potential shortcomings and failings. Practitioners should ensure that the full documentation is available. If the complaint response lists other documents, then copies of those items should be requested.

Various other matters may require further information to be provided. Sometimes this can take the form of the experience of the medic, or the experience of the medic in treating the specific condition.

Ongoing investigations

Unless a full admission on breach of duty and causation has been given by the defendant(s), it is prudent for liability investigations to remain a live issue during the lifespan of the stroke case. Although Part 31 Disclosure and Inspection of documents under CPR 1998 confirms the duty within standard disclosure includes providing documents which adversely affect a parties' own case, it is not uncommon for documents to be identified after expert evidence has been exchanged or close to trial. The duty of disclosure continues until the proceedings are concluded so the pursuit of any documents contended as ordinarily being available should not be abandoned.

Witness evidence

Obtaining preliminary proofs of evidence surrounding the circumstances and contended facts can be performed at various junctures with stroke claims, as in other clinical negligence matters. It can assist to obtain initial draft witness evidence relatively swiftly from the claimant (if possible) and any other relevant witnesses. This evidence will often need to be updated as matters develop and new information becomes available. Keep in mind that the claimant may have sustained a significant brain injury from stroke (and in some cases will lack capacity) and they may struggle with memory and cognition. Undertake investigations into potential witnesses. Obtain information and draft statements as part of the investigative process.

As the claim progresses, if witness statements are exchanged between the parties, it will be beneficial to reflect on whether any witnesses from the opponent(s) are possibly omitted. In certain circumstances, a court may be entitled to draw adverse inferences from the absence or silence of a witness who might be expected to have material evidence to give on an issue. See *Wisniewski v Central Manchester Health Authority* [1998] PIQR P324 at P340. The Supreme Court has commented on adverse inferences and *Wisniewski* in an employment case, *Efobi v Royal Mail Group Ltd*

[2021] UKSC 33 when Lord Leggatt JSC (with whom the other judges agreed) observed:

"The question of whether an adverse inference may be drawn from the absence of a witness is sometimes treated as a matter governed by legal criteria, for which the decision of the Court of Appeal in [Wisniewski] is often cited as authority. Without intending to disparage the sensible statements made in that case, I think there is a risk of making overly legal and technical what really is or ought to be just a matter of ordinary rationality. So far as possible, tribunals should be free to draw, or to decline to draw, inferences from the facts of the case before them using their common sense without the need to consult law books when doing so."

Summary

Performing thorough ongoing investigations, subject to proportionality, is an essential part of analysing a stroke claim. There could be an array of documentation to explore, obtain, review and scrutinise. Once all the available pieces of information are assessed, a further risk assessment as to the merits of the case can be performed. In summary, some key features of stroke investigations can include:

- From the outset, keep alert to the possibility that the case could be a failure to prevent stroke occurring, even if the claimant's initial instructions are concerns surrounding the events immediately after the stroke.

- Although some of the medical records may be challenged as inaccurate, treat them as a generally accurate and contemporaneous account of what occurred.

- The caveat to the above is, scrutinise records carefully with the claimant/witnesses.

- Develop an accurate chronology / timeline of events.

- Create a summary of key findings from the medical records review.

- Research any relevant Handbooks or similar.

- Scrutinise any policies relating to the issues.

- Consider any applicable national and/or local guidelines.

- Disclosure is an ongoing process and if liability is subsequently denied, further investigations may be required.

- Witness evidence will usually be necessary to obtain and be kept updated.

CHAPTER THREE

EXPERT EVIDENCE ON LIABILITY

For simplicity, the word liability is used in this chapter to encompass breach of duty and causation. There are elements surrounding expert evidence that equally apply to prognosis and quantum but the spotlight here is on key themes and issues with liability expert evidence in stroke claims.

The fundamental principles

The importance of expert evidence and the principles laid out by Creswell J in "*The Ikarian Reefer*" (*National Justice Compania Naviera SA v Prudential Assurance Co Ltd*) [1993] 2 Lloyd's Rep 68 cannot be overstated for a stroke claim. The value of obtaining evidence from competent, eminent experts can make or break cases. It is useful to remind experts that they should be familiar with CPR Part 35 and their obligations to the court.

Independent experts are fundamental to the process of clinical negligence claims. There are outstanding experts preparing reports but there are occasions where some experts have not satisfactorily addressed the issue of applying the legal principles. The courts will often begin a judgment in stroke (and other) claims with reference to the long-established *Bolam* test, which has been applied for almost 70 years. It is the most important case on liability in clinical negligence. It is necessary to apply the test in every case.

In *Bolam v Friern Hospital Management Committee* [1957] 1 WLR 582 McNair J set out what became known as 'the *Bolam* test' for breach of duty in clinical negligence cases. The judge stated:

> "*The test is the standard of the ordinary skilled man exercising and professing to have that special skill. A man need not possess the highest expert skill; it is well established law that it is sufficient if he exercises the ordinary skill of an ordinary competent man exercising that particular art.*"

The critical aspect was then delivered:

> "*A doctor is not guilty of negligence if he has acted in accordance with a practice accepted as proper by a responsible body of medical men skilled in that particular art... Putting it the other way round, a man is not negligent, if he is acting in accordance with such a practice, merely because there is a body of opinion who would take a contrary view.*"

In applying the *Bolam* test, the question is whether no reasonably competent clinician would have acted and exercised judgement in the way in which the clinician(s) did. Relevant standards by which the clinician is to be judged are the standards of the day. Differences of opinion and practice exist and will always exist in clinical/medical and other professions. A court may prefer one body of opinion to another but that is no basis for a finding of negligence. This is highlighted in *Maynard v West Midlands Regional Health Authority* [1984] 1 WLR 634 at 638E when Lord Scarman set out:

> "*... a judge's 'preference' for one body of distinguished professional opinion to another also professionally distinguished is not sufficient to establish negligence in a practitioner whose actions have received the seal of approval of those whose opinions, truthfully expressed, honestly held, were not preferred.*"

Further, in *Newell v Goldenberg* [1995] 6 Med LR Mantell J confirmed that:

> "*The Bolam principle provides a defence for those who lag behind the times. It cannot serve those who know better.*"

In the *Marion O'Brien* case (referred to within "policies and protocols" in chapter two), whilst not a stroke case, it begins with a recital of the *Bolam/Bolitho* principles demonstrating that it is often the starting point for a judge. It is the judge that determines whether an expert opinion is logical and supported by a body of peers. When expert evidence is tested at trial, the issues are for the judge to decide, taking into account all the evidence. In making the assessment of an expert's opinion, consideration will be given to:

- Whether the evidence is tendered in good faith.

- Whether the expert is responsible, competent and/or respectable.

- Whether the opinion is reasonable and has a logical basis. *Bolitho v City and Hackney Health Authority* [1998] AC 232 sets out this key principle.

The above (summarised) factors are eloquently set out by Green J in *C v Cumbria University Hospitals NHS Trust* [2014] EWHC 61 where it was affirmed:

> "*It is therefore insufficient for a Claimant to demonstrate only that there exists a body of competent expert opinion which disagrees with the judgment which was taken upon the facts of the present case. This is no more than a recognition of the fact that in an area where professionals exercise a high degree of technical and medical expertise that there may be a range of different views all of which might quite legitimately be held about the same matter. Accordingly, if there exists a body of competent professional expert opinion which supports the decision as reasonable in the circumstances it matters not that other experts might disagree… the task of the court is to see beyond stylistic blemishes and to concentrate upon the pith and substance of the expert opinion and to then evaluate its content against the evidence as a whole and thereby assess its logic.*"

It is trite law in clinical negligence that there may be a range of reasonable professional expert opinion on how to deal with each person in a given scenario. Experts should always apply the *Bolam/Bolitho* test to the matter at hand and give opinion on whether the professionals alleged to be negligent had acted in accordance with a responsible body of medical opinion within the relevant discipline. Experts should understand and be able to explain the fundamental principles and their application in stroke cases.

Approaching experts

Like other cases of alleged clinical negligence, experts should be carefully selected in stroke claims. Whilst applying the overarching principle of proportionality, determining which expert, and the disciplines of expertise to prepare initial reports assists in expediting matters. For some practitioners, collecting expert evidence begins with a breach of duty report. This may be suitable for a stroke case but instances arise where instructing a causation expert first may assist in accelerating the decision making on a stroke case.

There are times when a competent expert can give opinion on causation of a stroke case without having a separate breach of duty report/opinion available. To help achieve this, provide the expert with a suitable timeline/chronology and identification of key issues on potential breach of duty. This can enable the causation expert to give their opinion against those scenarios. Stroke cases that might fall into this category could include:

- Those with a modest value.
- Cases of alleged delay or failure to provide thrombolysis following a non-negligent stroke.
- Where breach of duty admissions are likely to be made or have been made.

- Where breach of duty might be confined to a narrow issue.

There can be numerous reasons to approach and instruct a causation expert first in a stroke case. When approaching experts in this regard, explain that a breach of duty report has not yet been obtained to ensure the expert is confident in preparing the first report. The expert will likely need a sufficiently detailed summary and chronology within the approach to establish that they have the relevant expertise. Some experts might give a preliminary 'steer' on whether they think the case has any prospects if a suitably prepared approach is provided.

When choosing breach of duty and causation experts, the process is akin to other clinical negligence cases. Ensure that the expert's CV being reviewed is up-to-date and check the expert has relevant expertise and experience to address the issues in the specific matter. It can be helpful to ask them directly. Some takeaway aspects, in addition to the usual criteria are:

- Identifying they have adequate experience in practice and in medico-legal reporting.
- That they have relevant expertise with the particular issue.
- That they have relevant credentials and accreditations.

For stroke cases, the (ordinarily) key summary details to include within an approach to a medical expert, especially for a causation report, will include amongst other things:

- The age / date of birth of the claimant and their gender.
- The claimant's pre-existing medical history synopsis. In particular, any cardiovascular disease, diabetes, any previous stroke details, excess alcohol/drug/smoking consumption.

- Their BMI and any family history of stroke or of note.
- Their pre-stroke medication chronology.
- A chronology with timeline of events leading up to the stroke, the day of the stroke itself, and consequences of the stroke.

A neurologist and/or stroke physician

It would very unusual if a stroke case did not involve either, an expert neurologist, or stroke physician. Or on rare occasions, both fields of expertise. It is a crucial area in any stroke claim and usually the leading expert for the case on causation and sometimes breach of duty too. It can be contended (in stroke cases) that a neurologist is a different discipline to that of a stroke physician. There are sub-specialities of expertise within neurology and stroke medicine so when dealing with causation of stroke, it will be an important consideration to determine the precise specialism of the stroke expert to instruct. Further, to scrutinise the opponent's expert, should liability/causation be disputed.

As outlined in chapter one, a neurologist or stroke physician will usually be the primary physician/clinician to manage a person that has sustained a stroke. Subject to the issues at hand in a case, parties can contend that one, or both, experts in this regard are required to give opinion in the matter. This point can be a tactical decision and one to further the position of the respective party. For example, if a claimant suffered a stroke that was allegedly negligent and should have been avoided, a stroke physician may be argued to be the suitable expert to report on causation. However, if the claimant had pre-existing health issues (perhaps muscular sclerosis) that fall under the remit of a neurologist, it may be necessary for a neurologist to report on causation and/or causation as to condition and prognosis. This would be to set out causation and/or the claimant's future non-negligent trajectory in light of the particular characteristics of their underlying (non-negligent) neurological condition. Nevertheless, it is far more common that only one expert in this regard will be permitted by the court to report on liability/causation.

Therefore, there is often a key choice from the outset of whether to instruct a neurologist or a stroke physician (or very occasionally both). Scrutinising the CV of the proposed expert is required to glean their practice and any sub-specialisms. These sub-specialisms should be carefully checked. Some neurologists will have extensive experience of managing stroke; others will not. Some neurologists are generalised in their practice and some will have sub-specialisms in other matters; for example, epilepsy. It would not be unusual for a neurologist to have limited experience of managing stroke and having limited bespoke expertise in stroke medicine.

Understanding the experts' frequency and regularity of managing the issue at hand is important to explore. It is useful to rigorously test an expert's specific expertise to clarify that they have good familiarity with the claimant's condition and issues arising in the case. It would be unwise to instruct the same expert on every stroke case.

It is recognised that there is a paucity of neurologists and stroke physicians in the UK so options may be limited in the choice of expert. Nevertheless, carefully selecting an expert most suitable for the case goes a long way. Given the huge annual incidence of stroke, it is noteworthy that there is only a small pool of experts that will have sufficient experience of stroke, alongside preparing Part 35 expert reports.

To further emphasise the point about whether to instruct a neurologist or stroke physician, a return to *Pickering* (referred to in chapter one when discussing heparin) is applicable. The defendant had contended that the claimant's general neurologist expert was not properly qualified to give opinion on causation. Their expert was a stroke physician, who could allegedly deal with the specific issue (being the potential of the left atrial blood clot(s) to embolise). The judgment does not give conclusions on this distinct point (and the claimant was successful) but it is evident that parties can seek to attack the suitability of a neurologist and/or stroke physician if they determine that the opposing expert does not have the necessary expertise or experience of addressing the issue(s) in question.

In *Runciman (Executor of the Estate of Susan Alexander Deceased) v University Hospital Southampton NHS Trust* [2024] EWHC 1800 (KB) the claim was dismissed as there was no breach of duty and even if breach had been established, causation would have failed in any event. The claimant suffered a cerebral venous sinus thrombosis (CVST) and it was alleged that her condition was misdiagnosed as an arterial ischaemic stroke (AIS) (both are types of stroke) which led to thrombolysis being administered. The former, CVST, is caused by a blood clot which occurs in the cerebral venous system whereas the latter, AIS, occurs in the arterial system. It was held that the diagnosis was a reasonable one to make at the time, whilst seen to be incorrect in hindsight. CVST is rare and there was an urgency to the situation to administer thrombolysis quickly and the claimant's presentation was deemed consistent with AIS. Various medical papers were adduced in evidence relating to these types of stroke. It was agreed that diagnosing and treating any stroke is urgent; that for AIS, treatment with thrombolysis improves outcomes and must take place within a window of 4.5 hours from the onset of the focal neurological symptoms.

In *Runciman* the claimant relied upon a neurologist whereas the defendant relied upon a stroke physician. Neil Moody KC, sitting as a Deputy High Court judge, was satisfied:

> "*that both experts were suitably qualified and experienced to give expert evidence on breach and causation.*"

This exemplifies that the court will evaluate and scrutinise the expertise of the neurologist/stroke physician relied upon by the parties.

Some elements to evaluate when selecting a neurologist/stroke physician are:

- Does the expert treat people that have sustained a stroke.

- If so, how many patients do they treat weekly/annually.
- Is their practice on the NHS and/or private (usually more relevant for breach of duty considerations).
- For how many years have they treated stroke patients.
- Do they sub-specialise in stroke and/or other matters.
- Do they have any publications such as books or literature articles and journals and if so, are they relevant to the issue(s).
- Are they part of any stroke committees or similar bodies.
- What experience of writing expert reports on stroke do they have.

When identifying the neurologist/stroke physician expert to report on liability, whether it be on breach of duty and/or causation, it assists to factor in their geographical proximity to the claimant. This expert may be required to prepare a report on condition and prognosis so determining whether they can travel to visit the claimant, or vice versa, is a matter to take into account. Consideration of proportionality will be needed again to assess whether it is proportionate for the expert to travel to visit the claimant. Balanced with this will be the need to avoid any potential conflict of interest for the expert (if a geographically local expert is instructed) and checking whether the claimant is physically able to travel to the proposed expert's clinic location (if a face-to-face appointment is required – which often will be the case).

Finally, most instructions to stroke experts to undertake a condition and prognosis appointment will be after a causation report has been prepared so it is known whether there are merits in the case. However, some experts might express a need to examine the claimant to complete a causation report in certain circumstances. Having a good line of ongoing communication with the expert is beneficial for scenarios like this to better understand why it might be required.

Instructing experts

Practitioners may have "in-house" preferences and styles for instructing experts. Some may limit the number of specific questions raised so the expert sets out their opinion without having a focus on the queries made. Others may have copious questions. There will then be others anywhere in between. For stroke, detailing the timeline and setting out issues for consideration is likely to assist an expert to have a laser focus on matters.

Experts can be instructed to draft full reports or other types of report, such as a "screening report" to assess whether it is a case which broadly has prospects of success. Should the report be supportive, then a more detailed or full report can be obtained when suitable. It can be helpful to send a copy of the proposed letter of instruction to the claimant prior to instructing an expert. They may have useful incites that they want to add or adjust and have specific questions they would like to be addressed. It is, after all, their case and giving them the opportunity to input into the instructions can be a beneficial exercise.

Stroke claims are not distinguishable from other clinical negligence cases in respect of the sequencing for instructing experts. Although a causation report could feasibly be obtained before a breach of duty report, experts will be instructed in the most organic fashion for the specific case. It can be helpful to communicate with the expert(s) beforehand to check they are able to provide comprehensive opinion without another discipline of report being needed beforehand. For example, if a causation expert would benefit from knowing what an expert neuroradiologist opines about specific scans, or what scans would likely have shown if they were not performed, it may be more effective and efficient to obtain the neuroradiology report before that causation expert is instructed.

Liability/causation disciplines

Common disciplines of expertise that may be required to report on liability/causation in stroke cases can include, in no particular order:

- Accident and Emergency
- Cardiology
- GP
- Haematology
- Neuroradiology
- Neurologist and/or stroke physician
- Neurosurgeon
- Paramedic
- Vascular

Each case inevitably requires its own determination of the necessary disciplines of expertise. For stroke, the commonly instructed experts on causation are likely to be a neurologist and/or stroke physician, neuroradiologist, neurosurgeon, vascular surgeon, haematologist and cardiologist. The other disciplines referred to above are likely to be limited to breach of duty. There will of course be many other disciplines of experts that could be required to report on liability in stroke claims. When considering causation, as advanced techniques and practices continually develop for stroke medicine, consider whether the expert has contemporaneous experience and up to date knowledge of relevant literature. If the expert has retired from clinical practice, probe how they are keeping up to date.

Experts and expert reports

The expert evidence produced is central to any clinical negligence claim. Significant time will be spent instructing and communicating with experts, reviewing their evidence, advising on the evidence, discussing matters, updating evidence, and sometimes challenging the evidence. Strong, constructive relationships can be developed with experts and these productive relationships will assist cases being investigated thoroughly. Nevertheless, the obligation of an expert is to the court.

Holding conferences with experts, often with counsel, is a useful exercise in stroke claims. Under cross examination (at trial), experts may be asked by opposing counsel to explain the test for breach of duty and causation. If an expert cannot soundly explain the legal tests, then a judge is likely to be unimpressed and their opinion will be carefully evaluated. An expert that is entrenched in their opinion will probably not make for an impressive witness to the judge.

Experts should be able to entertain consideration of differing views and explain matters carefully and calmly. Experts that are unwilling to engage in dialogue surrounding alternative options or opinions may face the judge concluding their opinion is too rigid and thus, undermine the credibility of their evidence. Accordingly, having conferences can unveil their opinion in more detail and provide the platform for a candid symposium on the issues.

Experts should not be advocates for their instructing party. It will be of concern if an expert is inconsistent. Often, the only way that expert opinion can be forensically analysed without a trial is by conference(s). Challenging expert opinion is a necessary part of reviewing a stroke claim. Again, in the claimant's successful case of *Pickering*, Ritchie J found the defendant's haematology experts' oral evidence to be inconsistent with their report. It is incumbent to forensically analyse the expert evidence and apply rigour to ensure reports are appropriately completed before they are served/disclosed.

At trial, the judge will more likely be persuaded by experts that are:

- Balanced;
- Accurate;
- Convincing;
- Reliable;
- Consistent;
- Acknowledging;
- Cogent;
- Impressive;
- Extensively experienced with the issue.

The language described above is often applied by judges to distinguish their preference from one expert to another of the same discipline. Stroke cases will often require expert evidence to be updated regularly across various disciplines of medicine when new information and other reports become available. Finalised reports need to be sufficiently detailed, setting out the issues with narrative analysis on how the expert's opinion has been formulated.

Medical literature

Stroke claims will often have various studies and literature references contained within the liability/causation expert evidence and this would ultimately be meticulously analysed at trial. Experts should be able to clearly explain relevant literature in their application to the individual stroke case. If the literature is not provided with their report, a copy of the articles or papers referred to should be obtained and reviewed. Understanding how the medical paper(s) are applicable to the specific case is important in stroke claims. At joint statements in litigation, experts are ordered to produce relevant aspects of literature upon which they rely. If the first time a study is known at joint statements, this can create further investigations and potentially impact a case.

A compelling expert should be able to explain medical literature in a manner that legal practitioners and judges can readily understand and how it supports or is unsupportive of the case. Spending time addressing this is a worthwhile exercise. Returning to *Pickering*, Ritchie J gave a forensic examination of the literature and had plainly carefully scrutinised the available evidence. This judgment is an example of how medical literature will be rigorously evaluated in stroke cases to assist in determining causation, and particularly when the available medical literature does not contain studies that directly correlate with the liability/causation issue at hand. This can be a common feature of stroke litigation; as stroke, despite its prevalence, has so many variables and factors, that the medical literature may not closely correspond with the issues in the case. Therefore, it is important to investigate and probe the expert opinion in relation to the literature that is relied upon, its relevance or otherwise, and to analyse interpretations of the literature or data when liability/causation is in issue. Some of the more commonly cited literature for causation in stroke claims is highlighted in chapter five.

Agendas and joint discussions

Should agendas and joint discussions by experts be required, then *Saunders v Central Manchester University Hospitals NHS Foundation Trust* [2018] EWHC 343 conveys that parties should agree a single agenda. Further, agendas should narrow issues and not be "*an overly lawyered document*" as described by Master Cook in *Aderounmu v Colvin* [2021] EWHC 2293 when echoing Yip J in *Saunders*.

Interestingly, *Aderounmu* was a stroke case of an alleged GP failure to refer the claimant following suspected stroke. The issue to be determined surrounded the claimant's capacity to conduct litigation and limitation. The court was required to determine as a preliminary issue whether the claim was statute barred. Master Cook held in favour of the claimant as the approach to mental capacity to litigate was issue specific; see also *Masterman-Lister v Jewell* [2022] EWCA Civ 1889. An individual might have subject matter capacity but not litigation capacity and the court is not bound by the expert evidence alone; it can take into account all the available evidence.

Agendas are not always necessary in stroke litigation. They can be helpful in many cases and assist to tease out pivotal issues on breach/causation but there will be some cases where they are not helpful; and experts can discuss and prepare their joint statement(s) without an agenda. Consider whether an agenda is required and communicate with the expert(s) and opposing parties. Do not simply default to drafting them.

Summary

Liability/causation expert evidence is often a complex area in stroke claims. A summarised reflection is:

- Apply the *Bolam/Bolitho* test to each case.
- Scrutinise the CV and experience of experts before instructing them to report on liability.
- Assess whether a neurologist and/or stroke physician is best suited for the case.
- For breach of duty, consider experts that are best placed with the particular experience to opine on practice at the time of the events occurring.

- For causation, as advanced techniques and practices continually develop for stroke, consider an expert that has contemporaneous experience or can be shown to be up to date with their knowledge.

- Analyse the sequence of reports to obtain if a number of reports are likely needed and keep proportionality in mind.

- Expert evidence will often need to be updated. When a new report arrives, think whether existing reports need updating.

- Ensure experts take into account all the components as the evidence develops.

- Where possible, review any relevant literature and seek to understand its relevance.

- Test whether the expert can explain in straight forward terms the relevance of literature to the case.

- Examine the expert evidence rigorously before finalising reports to ensure they are as robust as possible.

- Ensure experts understand the fundamental legal principles surrounding the *Bolam*/*Bolitho* tests.

- The question as to whether breach of duty is established is ultimately a matter for the court and not the experts.

- Consider the coherence and logic of any expert opinion.

- Apply the same extensive rigour when reviewing any evidence of the opponent and joint statements, and test matters further with your own expert(s).

CHAPTER FOUR

BREACH OF DUTY

Broad considerations in respect of breach of duty for stroke cases are revealed here. As addressed in the previous chapter, expert evidence will ordinarily be required. Like other clinical negligence claims allegedly causing neurological and/or neuropsychological injuries or similar, the potential acts or omissions can span across a myriad of branches of medicine and clinical disciplines. It would be an impossible and unwieldy task to try and cover the vast array of potential breach of duty scenarios and all the different types of stroke. Instead, the focus is on general themes and areas within stroke claims with example cases and practical points to consider.

Identifying potential breaches

Give consideration in each case as to whether the stroke should have been avoided in the first place before potentially moving on to the management following stroke. It might help to identify all the disciplines of clinicians that reviewed the claimant before the stroke and on the day of stroke to indicate what fields of expertise could be required for expert reports.

If there is complaint documentation, DATIX or similar information available, a potential breach may be identified at an earlier stage than the expert report(s). In seeking to reduce time and costs, on appropriate cases, the proposed defendant(s) can be invited to admit breach of duty based on the available documentation/evidence and to commence causation investigations.

As explained in chapters one and two, undertaking a careful analysis of the medical records and having a grasp of stroke, together with common issues surrounding stroke prevention and stroke medicine, are beneficial in directing efforts to investigate areas for potential breach of duty allegations. As can often occur in clinical negligence claims, there can be breach but no causation and practitioners will have their own preferences with addressing the chronology of breach. Stroke claims can be notoriously demanding in terms of aligning causation with potential breach of duty. Therefore, if there are potential breaches of duty ranging across multiple expert disciplines and dates, it may be appropriate to concurrently investigate causation to try and minimise the prospect of extensive breach research but there being no causation.

Types of stroke

Ischaemic

As the incidence of ischaemic stroke is far more commonplace than haemorrhagic stroke, it is reasonable to conclude that investigating this type of stroke will be more typical. Breach of duty could arise from many scenarios. Keep in mind the clinicians involved prior to the stroke. In *Tucker v Griffiths* [2016] EWHC 1214 (QB) the claimant had an acute ischaemic stroke secondary to infective endocarditis. There was an alleged failure by the defendant GP to suspect infective endocarditis and refer the claimant to hospital. Breach of duty was denied. Causation was accepted and quantum was agreed, subject to the finding of breach of duty. The court accepted that the defendant had infective endocarditis in mind as a possible, if unlikely diagnosis, and that it was reasonable to direct the claimant for another appointment, rather than making an urgent referral to hospital and the claim was dismissed. Other cases of infective endocarditis referred to are *Lyndon* and *McCabe.*

TIA

TIA can be an early warning sign for risk of stroke. The risk is at its highest in the initial days and weeks after TIA. Common features in respect of breach of duty where a TIA occurred prior to stroke includes consideration of:

- Were the symptoms described likely to be TIA. Some claims may fail on the basis that it was not deemed to be TIA.

- Should TIA have been suspected based on the symptoms.

- If it was TIA, what, if any, management was then required.

- Management often includes an urgent referral to a TIA clinic for tests and checks. Issues can arise as to the speed of being seen in a TIA clinic.

- If the claimant was not given medication following TIA, usually aspirin, then an issue can be whether this should have been given. However, sometimes there can be contraindications to prescribing this.

Haemorrhagic

Although on the face of some claims, it can appear that there were potential failings in diagnosing/referring/delaying/other matters with haemorrhagic stroke, such as subarachnoid haemorrhage, cases can frequently fail on their facts. In claims for alleged failings surrounding diagnosis/treatment and so on of subarachnoid haemorrhage, some potential points to consider can include:

- Were symptoms of sudden and severe headache reported to the clinician(s).

- What other symptoms were reported and do they fit the 'classic' type of symptoms.
- Had there been other complaints/symptoms in their history such as previous head injury that were not investigated.
- Was the presentation of symptoms likely to be an emergency requiring immediate transfer/admission to hospital.
- Was there a CT scan performed and was it reported adequately.
- Was a referral made to the neurosurgery team. If so, what was the suitable timeframe to have acted upon it.
- Was surgery necessary if it had not been performed.
- If surgery had been undertaken, was the surgery of an acceptable standard.
- Diagnosing subarachnoid haemorrhage is not always straightforward as symptoms such as headache are very common so witness evidence and expert evidence will both be crucial.

Breach of duty was denied in *Jaciubek v Gulati & Anor* [2016] EWHC 269 (QB). Here, there was an alleged failure to identify or act on signs of a subarachnoid haemorrhage by the GP and then again by the clinician in the A&E assessment. The case failed on the facts. The claimant failed to establish the alleged complaints history. As described in chapter one, in *Holt v Edge*, a GP was not negligent for failing to diagnose a subarachnoid haemorrhage and refer the claimant to hospital sooner when the claimant had not presented with the usual symptoms. The things to consider will also apply to cases of intracerebral haemorrhage.

Hypertension

If the claimant had been diagnosed with hypertension prior to stroke, then consider whether the NICE guidelines were followed. Review whether the monitoring of hypertension fell within the guidelines and any relevant Handbook(s) (usually the GP Handbook is the most relevant). Consider if hypertension was a risk factor; this is especially relevant for lacunar strokes and intracranial haemorrhage.

If the claimant had not been diagnosed with hypertension, review whether there were opportunities prior to stroke that should have led to this diagnosis. Further, consider if the monitoring of complaints was satisfactory. This could include blurred vision, chest pain and headaches.

If blood pressure (BP) readings for the claimant were equal or higher than 140/90 in the medical records then question whether the BP readings should have led to a diagnosis of hypertension. Compiling a list of blood pressure readings and blood pressure reviews may shine further light on the overall picture.

Atrial fibrillation (AF)

As outlined in chapter one, AF is the most common heart rhythm disturbance and having this condition poses a risk of stroke. It is therefore likely to be considered a common condition that clinicians should be familiar with and provide a proactive management and treatment plan. If a claimant had a CHA_2DS_2-VASc risk score but anticoagulation had not been considered or offered by clinician(s), then it would be something to investigate as the only effective measure to reduce the risk of ischaemic stroke in AF is anticoagulation.

If the claimant had AF and had an ischaemic stroke, things to consider may include:

- Was AF already diagnosed; was it a risk factor.

- Were NICE guidelines followed.

- Was anticoagulation started.

- Was the claimant compliant with taking their medication i.e. had it been prescribed, would they have likely taken it as directed. A claim may fail if it cannot be demonstrated that the claimant would have taken medication – for example, if they were non-compliant with other medication.

- Were there any earlier opportunities to diagnose AF and give medication.

- Was the control/monitoring of anticoagulation/other medication adequate.

Thrombolysis

Intravenous thrombolytic therapy remains the guideline-recommended treatment to try and improve outcomes after acute ischaemic stroke. Thrombolysis commonly features as an issue (that is frequently disputed) relating to breach of duty. There can be contended failures to provide it (if not given). Usually due to alleged delays in the pathway/diagnosis of stroke or it was deemed unsuitable, or to provide it as quickly as it should have been. Further and conversely, allegations can be that it should not be given in certain circumstances. For example, there are contraindications in its use such as a claimant with prior or acute intracranial haemorrhage and active bleeding (see *Runciman* in chapter three by way of example).

Whether thrombolysis is given to a child will depend on the circumstances but it is not standard treatment for children (neither is thrombectomy). The guidelines for stroke in childhood outline that thrombolysis could be given to children age eight and over and may be considered for those age two to eight. It will be a case-by-case basis so establishing breach of duty for failing to give thrombolysis to a child can be more challenging than that of adult stroke.

If the claim surrounds a non-negligent stroke having occurred and the management post-stroke is in issue, the crucial breach factor will often be akin to addressing:

- (If eligible for it) what was the latest non-negligent time that thrombolysis should have been given.

As set out in chapter one, the timeline to receive thrombolysis is very acute. There is normally a maximum window of 4.5 hours from onset of symptoms in which thrombolysis can be given.

Before thrombolysis can be administered there will need to be an assessment and diagnosis, then a CT head scan. The CT scan will be reported and reviewed as to whether this demonstrates signs of stroke. It should be performed quickly. A normal CT scan does not exclude an ischaemic stroke but it does exclude a haemorrhagic stroke.

Once a claimant arrives at hospital following stroke (unless the stroke occurs in hospital) to the latest non-negligent time that thrombolysis needs to occur, may have a range of expert opinion (subject to them being a suitable candidate to receive it). Claimants may argue it should be less than 45 minutes, or less than one hour pursuant to the SNAP data and Rudd. Defendants may contend that one hour or less is not feasible and it was not a breach of duty if it took longer than that. Each case will require factual considerations to include issues such as:

- The availability of performing the CT scan.

- The condition of the claimant and assessing them.

- Undertaking any other potential tests.

- Any relevant policies.

Consideration of the 'door to needle' time of intervention may need review for breach of duty. Hyper-acute stroke units might work nearer to a 30-minute time target to give thrombolysis, whereas other hospitals may take one hour or a bit longer. Many stroke units have the initial drug bolus dose prepared while the CT scan is being undertaken and the bolus is then given within the scanner.

The timescale of one hour may have the potential to be deemed reasonable but once the time exceeds one hour, then extra scrutiny as to whether this is a breach of duty is required. Broad-brush, the usual timeline for a claimant to arrive in hospital with a potential concern for stroke to giving thrombolysis generally varies in expert opinion between the region of around 30 minutes to 75-90 minutes maximum.

There is literature (The Lancet by Campbell et al 2019) that explores extending the thrombolysis window from 4.5 to 9 hours. However, most NHS Trusts do not give thrombolysis after 4.5 hours. It is not common practice within England and Wales to extend the thrombolysis period and it would be challenging to establish there being a breach of duty for not giving thrombolysis after the 4.5 hour window expired.

There can be disputes on thrombolysis not being given if clinicians deemed it unsuitable and decided against its use. Some stroke clinicians do not administer thrombolysis to people with mild stroke but some will do. Those that do might explain, for example, it is because the person has isolated loss of vision or dysphasia that are considered severe defects despite them not increasing the NIHSS to greater than four. Thrombolysis might be given for mild stroke on the basis that the risk of haemorrhage, particularly in young people, is not high and there might be some benefit to the treatment.

Thrombolysis is cautioned when a chronic infarct is reported on the CT scan. Even if a new acute infarct is present on CT scan there could be a reasonable body of clinicians that would not administer thrombolysis in this setting. Also, it would unlikely be administered with rapidly resolving stroke.

A summary of thrombolysis as a breach of duty issue includes:

- Thrombolysis cannot normally be given after 4.5 hours. If a claimant arrives at hospital 4 – 4.5 hours after stroke symptom onset and there are no failings on part of the Ambulance Services, then it is unlikely to be a breach of duty in not giving it.

- Was there a missed opportunity to give thrombolysis before the 4.5 hour window expired following onset of stroke.

- The timeline for arrival at hospital to giving thrombolysis could reasonably range between around 30 minutes to 75-90 minutes. It would be more difficult but still possible to establish breach of duty for failing to provide thrombolysis within 30-60 minutes of arrival at hospital.

- Was it contraindicated to give thrombolysis in the circumstances.

GPs

When working a full day, GPs will likely assess dozens of people. They will often be under pressure to diagnose, give advice, prescriptions, referrals, follow ups and other matters as necessary. Stroke claims against GPs can include a vast array of issues and the following are examples of potential shortcomings that could be a breach:

- Not recognising symptoms of a TIA and treating / referring accordingly.

- Not recognising symptoms of sudden temporary loss of vision through one (or both) eye(s), only lasting for a short time as potential amaurosis fugax and acting upon this.

- Not recognising / treating hypertension and other conditions that are risk factors for stroke.

- Not acting upon test results.

- Not making referrals, whether emergency / urgent / other to specialists such as neurology / vascular / ophthalmology / cardiology etc.

- There can be issues like systems errors such as failing to notify to make an appointment for tests.

Many stroke claims against GPs will be based upon the underpinning contention that they have missed the early warning indicators of stroke potentially occurring (or perhaps they did notice but the important issue is the actions/management thereafter). The main thrust can often surround alleged failings to prescribe blood thinning / clot busting medications and/or for failing to refer people to specialists / secondary care / tertiary services for further assessment and potential treatment. A breach of duty report from an expert GP can be a common part of investigating stroke claims.

As outlined earlier in this chapter, *Jaciubek v Gulati* and *Holt v Edge* were stroke claims against GPs that were unsuccessful. These cases indicate the importance of fact-finding and the evidence from the defendant GP may be persuasive. Similarly, in *Beech v Timney* [2013] EWHC 2345 (QB) despite the GP failing to conduct certain medical examinations on the claimant, who had complained of early morning headaches and then subsequently suffered a stroke, the court was satisfied that the GP had taken and recorded the claimant's blood pressure accurately prior to the stroke. After the claimant sustained their stroke, tests revealed he had very high blood pressure. The claimant alleged his blood pressure was probably significantly elevated when he was reviewed by the defendant and the recorded measurement (of a normal 110/80) was incorrect. Whilst the evidence demonstrated that in some respects the defendant fell short of the standard to be expected of a reasonably competent GP, those examples were not so glaring as to cast doubt on their ability to take and record a blood pressure measurement. This case further typifies that the court generally treats the medical records as being accurate.

McCabe v Moore (see chapter two) is an example of a successful claim against a GP, although the two other defendants were not in breach of duty. *McCabe* arguably typifies how some stroke claims against GPs have the common denominator of missing "red flags" and failing to refer.

Ambulance Services/Trusts

Claims against paramedics or the telephone operators usually fall to be pursued against the Ambulance Services/Trust. It is probable that three of the most frequent overarching allegations of breach of duty in stroke claims against the Ambulance Services are:

- Time delays. Such as the correct categorisation priority of an emergency call; the time it takes for the paramedics to arrive at the scene with the claimant; making a provisional diagnosis; and transporting the claimant to a suitable hospital.

- Failing to diagnose potential stroke during the assessment.

- Failing to diagnose (or consider) a condition that should have led to a referral for treatment for stroke risk.

Once a paramedic diagnoses stroke, they should, where possible, transport the person to a hyper-acute stroke unit as soon as possible. People that are taken to hospitals without stroke units or thrombectomy centres often need to be transferred to another hospital with a comprehensive stroke centre (CSC). This can mean they go back into the system as a category two call alongside other calls despite it being confirmed they are eligible for a thrombectomy. Whether the claimant was transported to the correct hospital in the circumstances can sometimes be a matter to review.

When allegations are that the telephone call operator failed to assign or code the call as urgent, the guidelines will often be the Trust's own guidelines. In each case, ensure these are reviewed.

The National Stroke Service Model sets out service outcomes for:

- 999 call categorisation.
- Pre-hospital triage.
- Transfer to a CSC. Of note, for people with ischaemic stroke, a call to needle time (thrombolysis) of 180 minutes is stated.

There are target response times for ambulances to arrive with a person. In England and Wales these are:

England, category two:	A serious condition, such as stroke which may require rapid assessment and/or urgent transport is 18 minutes.
Wales, category Amber:	There is no specific time for serious but not immediately life-threatening (patients who will often need treatment to be delivered on the scene and may then need to be taken to hospital).

Of note, Northern Ireland is also 18 minutes and Scotland is 19 minutes. If the proposed defendant is a Welsh Ambulance Service Trust, their national standards for target response times are silent which could make pursuing allegations for time delay more challenging. Additive to this, the response times are noted to be a target so not adhering to them is not in itself confirmation of a breach of duty. However, comparisons with the other nations could be a point to consider.

In England, the evidence is that it takes just over one hour on average from symptom onset before a call is made to the ambulance services (Dr Hargroves and Dr Lowe (2022) Stroke: GIRFT Programme National Specialty Report). Once the call is made, the average response time to emergencies like stroke was just over 41 minutes in 2021-22. In December 2022, the average length of time stroke patients had to wait for an ambulance was just over 90 minutes – more than five times the 18-minute target (NHS England (April 2022) Statistical Note: Ambulance Quality Indicators). The Ambulance Services will often be under pressure so whilst at first glance there could appear to be a time delay, all the circumstances are taken into account.

When assessing a person following a call to the emergency services for suspected stroke, the paramedic(s) should normally use a validated stroke screening tool. The FAST test (unilateral facial weakness, arm or leg weakness, speech disturbance) is the most commonly associated diagnosis for stroke but the FAST test does not identify everyone with acute stroke. People that are FAST negative but in whom stroke is still suspected should be treated as if they have stroke until the diagnosis has been excluded by a stroke clinician. Other signs and symptoms from suspected stroke can include:

- Sudden onset of dizziness.
- Confusion.
- Loss of consciousness for a short period of time.
- Severe headache with unknown cause.
- Altered gait.

- Difficulty speaking.

- Difficulty understanding.

Consider whether any of the above symptoms were present during the assessment.

Paramedic(s) failing to identify (potential) stroke diagnosis, or considering it and not transporting the claimant to hospital can be a potential breach of duty. Assess the notes made by the paramedic, cross referenced against the call log(s), any lay witness evidence and documentary evidence. If there are videos of the claimant (often mobile phone footage) then this can be compelling evidence of their symptoms/presentation.

If the paramedic(s) determine stroke as a possible diagnosis, consider the following:

- Whether they made a pre-alert call to the hospital they were transporting the claimant to. This can enable a pre-hospital triage supported by a stroke clinician to determine early identification of whether the person is a possible candidate for thrombolysis or thrombectomy.

- Whether they transported the claimant to the nearest CSC i.e. was the claimant taken to the most suitable hospital in the circumstances.

- The time taken from arrival at the scene of the claimant, to make a suspected diagnosis and arrival at hospital. Paramedics are to minimise time spent on scene if they suspect an acute stroke.

- Whether the notes made by the paramedic include time of symptom onset, their FAST assessment, affected side of weakness, blood pressure measurements and so on. Evaluate whether the notes are likely accurate and adequately detail sufficient information for the stroke clinician to utilise.

- What, if any, handover discussion occurred. Was a full and adequate handover made to the emergency department.

Accident and Emergency (A&E)

It is widely recognised that NHS A&E departments in England and Wales are under huge pressures. They deal with problems 24/7. There is no respite. The environment upon which clinicians and their colleagues work is probably only properly understood by those working within the NHS. Moving away from thrombolysis 'time-related' cases, many other instances can occur whereby clinicians in A&E review a person that has not suffered a stroke but subsequently goes on to do so. The duty to take reasonable care is applicable to all staff in A&E; clinicians or not; see *Darnley v Croydon Health Services NHS Trust* [2018] UKSC 50. Earlier attendances over the years at A&E should be readily considered as part of the breach of duty investigations.

An example is *Crammond v Medway* when the claimant suffered an ischaemic stroke secondary to acute coronary syndrome (ACS). The claimant had presented to A&E four years earlier complaining of chest pain and he was seen by a triage nurse. Following a normal ECG the A&E doctor chose not to review the claimant and instead, directed the claimant to be streamed to the same day treatment centre. Breach of duty was denied but the claimant succeeded as they were able to demonstrate they had presented with symptoms suggestive of ACS. There was a failure to illicit a history which would have led to their admission and appropriate treatment to avoid the subsequent stroke. The triage nurse had not been negligent but the A&E doctor had been.

Some trends for stroke breach of duty in A&E includes:

- Handover delays.

- Incorrect triage prioritisation.
- Delays in obtaining scans.
- Failures to illicit a suitable history.
- Failure to refer to the stroke unit/clinician at all, or in adequate time.
- Failure to review by a suitable clinician / discharging inappropriately.
- Delay in diagnosis / incorrect diagnosis.

<u>Hospital events and clinical disciplines</u>

Distinguishing A&E claims, when a claimant has suffered a stroke and was managed by clinicians (and the hospital Trust is the defendant) there is a plethora of situations for allegations arising due to substandard care. Some considerations are profiled below.

Surgery

If the claimant suffers a stroke during, or immediately following surgery, then extra scrutiny of the surgical and anaesthetic records is needed. In *Mills v Oxford University Hospitals NHS Trust* [2019] EWHC 936 (QB) the claimant suffered a haemorrhagic stroke secondary to alleged surgical negligence in connection with removal of a brain tumour by a neurosurgeon. There was a secondary allegation of failure to warn of the risk of surgery or provide advice of variant treatments. Interestingly, there was no negligence in the surgical performance but there was failure to obtain informed consent. Causation was established so the claim succeeded.

When reviewing the potential for breach of duty during surgery, sometimes there can be failures with the anaesthetic monitoring and implementation of anaesthesia which can result in stroke. For example, if a person's blood pressure is allowed to stay too low for too long during anaesthetic, causing hypotension, this can have an adverse outcome. If there is a prolonged reduction in the blood supply to the brain (and/or spinal cord) then a stroke/infarction can occur. Analyse the drug charts, blood pressure measurements before, during, and after surgery, and cross reference these to any guidelines such as the Association of Anaesthetists recommendations for standards of monitoring during anaesthesia and recovery.

Vascular

Vascular issues frequently arise within stroke litigation because disruption to the blood supply may lead to problems like deep vein thrombosis (DVT), pulmonary embolism and cerebrovascular accident which can cause stroke. Breach of duty from vascular problems will not be limited to vascular surgeons. Various clinicians treat people for complaints when there could be an underlying vascular problem that needs managing. Common components of these stroke claims include allegations of incorrect diagnosis, failing to treat/refer and surgical error.

In *Britchford v Staffordshire And Stoke-On-Trent Partnership NHS Trust* [2018] EWHC 2109 (QB) the claimant suffered an ischaemic stroke affecting the right basal ganglia. There was an alleged failure to suspect a new onset of a vascular problem affecting their right hand and wrist, rather than giving a diagnosis of tendonitis when the claimant attended a walk-in centre and was seen by a nurse practitioner. Breach of duty and causation were denied. The case failed on the facts. The account given by the claimant as to the appearance of their limb supporting vascular problems was rejected owing to inconsistency. The diagnosis of tendonitis and discharging them was reasonable in the circumstances.

In *Nicholas v Imperial College Healthcare NHS Trust* [2012] EWHC 591 (QB) a vascular surgeon's treatment and advice to the claimant who subsequently suffered a stroke was not negligent. The claimant had undergone surgery (carotid endarterectomy) but a follow-up scan revealed a residual flap in her artery. The claimant temporarily lost vision in one eye caused by a blood clot so a second surgery was performed. She suffered a stroke during this procedure. The first surgery was not substandard as the presence of the flap, despite being unusual, did not mean the procedure was performed below an acceptable standard. The claim was dismissed.

Radiology

Failing to report the CT/MRI/other scans correctly/adequately can potentially be a breach of duty. Some hospitals employ non-medical reporting radiographers. They are not trained to the level of a clinical radiologist. This can arguably create an environment whereby the interpretation and reporting of scans is not synonymous to what is expected of a reasonably competent clinical radiologist. An expert report is usually required to ascertain opinion on radiology breach of duty, if suspected. The report can also sometimes assist with opinion on causation.

Input from an interventional radiologist may have been required prior to stroke which can sometimes be a point to investigate on breach. For example, if the claimant should have undergone an embolization procedure prior to stroke, or to review whether the procedure was performed correctly. Embolization can be performed for various reasons such as slowing down blood flow and shrinking abnormal tissue by reducing its blood supply. This can be an alternative to surgery or a pre-surgical procedure. A report from an interventional radiologist can be needed on occasion.

Neurology

The claimant was unable to establish liability for avoiding their stroke in *Scott v Northern Devon Healthcare Trust* [2000] 7 WLUK 924. It was alleged that the defendant failed to refer the claimant to a neurologist after she complained of recurring dizzy spells and numbness. The treating clinician alleged to have been in breach was a general physician but the liability evidence of the neurologists at trial was relevant "*on the totality of the evidence.*" It was contended that had she been referred, she would have been prescribed warfarin treatment to prevent the stroke. Breach of duty was not established. Even with a referral to a neurologist, with the limited time available, the stroke would not have been avoided so causation would have failed.

As described previously, a neurologist (or stroke physician) will usually be the primary physician that a person is (or should have been) referred to for suspected risk of stroke. In claims of alleged failure to refer the claimant to a neurologist, expert opinion from the neurologist may be required on liability to confirm matters such as:

- Whether such a referral would have been accepted.
- The timescale that the claimant would have been examined by a neurologist.
- Any further tests/investigations needed.
- What diagnosis would have been given.
- Any treatment that would have been recommended.
- The totality of the picture/evidence.

Haematology

Haematology breach of duty (and causation issues) may arise in stroke claims because disorders/diseases of the blood can impact matters like the blood coagulation system and haemoglobin levels which might be associated with stroke. In respect of breach of duty allegations, the management of a haematological disorder may be the most prevalent issue arising and could require breach of duty opinion from various disciplines (not just haematology) such as a paediatrician if in relation to a child.

For example, in the paediatric stroke case of *ST v Maidstone and Tunbridge Wells NHS Trust* [2015] EWHC 51 (QB) there was an alleged failure to respond to and appropriately treat congenital haematological conditions. Liability evidence was given by haematologists and paediatricians (as well as neuroradiologists and (paediatric) neurologists). The claimant's pre-existing condition meant his haemoglobin levels required careful monitoring and he was prone to become anaemic. Breach of duty was partially admitted, whilst causation was denied. There was an admitted delay in admitting the claimant to hospital and performing a blood transfusion. The further (denied) allegations were failures to promptly administer intravenous fluids and give diuretics. Some breaches were established but causation failed. Causation in *ST* is considered in the next chapter.

Other

There will be many situations whereby stroke claims can be pursued (not necessarily successfully) in respect of breach of duty across branches of medicine/healthcare. This includes maternity care.

In *AB v East Lancashire Hospitals NHS Trust* [2019] EWHC 3542 (QB) there was an alleged failure in the claimant's mother's antenatal care allegedly causing a perinatal arterial ischaemic stroke (which was said to have occurred before the umbilical cord was cut). The claimant suffered with cerebral palsy amongst other disabilities. It was alleged that on two dates there were findings that mandated senior obstetric review for consultant led antenatal care. Breach of duty and causation were denied. The defendant contended that a finding of the retroplacental clot is common in the early weeks of pregnancy and even if a consultant had reviewed the scan findings, they would have referred the mother back to midwifery-led care. Causation was denied on the basis that the stroke was likely suffered in the neonatal period. The cases of *Bolam*, *Bolitho*, *Maynard* and *C v Cumbria* were cited by Lambert J when addressing breach of duty. Various guidelines were considered and the management/care was assessed as reasonable. The claim was dismissed on breach and causation.

A slightly unique case was *Sims v MacLennan* [2015] EWHC 2739 (QB). This was a Fatal Accidents Act claim arising from stroke. There was an alleged failure to provide advice to the deceased to have their blood pressure (BP) checked during a DVLA medical examination following a raised reading. Breach of duty and causation were denied. The case failed on the facts. The defendant was judged to have appropriately advised the deceased to attend his GP and have his BP checked. Further, even if there had been a failure, it was not causative of the death from stroke nine years later.

Summary of breach of duty

A vast range of expert disciplines can fall under the microscope for breach of duty in stroke claims. There are undoubtedly many more than have been described above. Determining where to focus and progress breach of duty issues can be a complex task. Consider the following:

- Identify the disciplines of clinicians that treated the claimant prior to their stroke (and following their stroke for good measure).

- Identify all the claimant's pre-existing conditions before their stroke and what branches of medicine these conditions may fall under.

- Carefully analyse what potential breach of duty expert reports might reasonably be required.

- Develop an accurate timeline on potential breach of duty if they span more than one.

- Consider whether the primary case is failure to avoid the stroke occurring.

- Apply forensic rigour to the *Bolam* and *Bolitho* tests.

- Assess whether breach of duty report(s) are needed prior to a causation report and the sequence of any further reports to obtain. This helps to try and avoid significant time investigating breach in case there is no causation.

CHAPTER FIVE

CAUSATION

The need to establish causation in stroke cases applies the same principles permeating across other clinical negligence cases. This chapter outlines matters with causation in stroke but as it can be so wide-ranging, a selection of issues are surveyed.

Seeking to simplify some key issues in each case can include the following:

Absent any breach of duty;

- Would the stroke have been avoided completely and if so, how and why.

- Would the effects of the stroke have been reduced resulting in a different condition and prognosis outcome and if so, how and why.

Overview

Causation in clinical negligence claims often raises difficult and complex aspects of law. Indeed, entire books are written on causation and material contribution alone. Eminent academics and practitioners publish papers on causation that are very informative. A broad overview summary of causation for stroke claims is outlined but it is often an especially difficult issue to grapple with and each case will need its own scrutiny.

The 'but for' test can be applied to many clinical negligence claims and this is usually the initial approach to consider for causation in a stroke claim. The basic principle is that a claimant can recover damages for injuries if they can prove that the breach of duty was the cause of injury and but for the breach, the injury would have been avoided. The claimant will need to establish the nature and extent of the injury arises from the breach and what would have occurred but for (or 'absent') the breach of duty. The determination is made on the balance of probabilities (51% or more). In applying the but for test it will be assumed that the defendant would have acted non-negligently (see *Bolitho*).

Where the but for principle for causation cannot be established, causation can be proved when the negligence of the defendant has materially contributed to the injury. In cases where there is more than one cause of the damage, it is usually sufficient to prove the defendant's breach was a cause of the loss, even if it was not the main or sole cause. However, importantly, the defendant's breach needs to be more than minimal (de minimis) and needs to be proved that it was material. Proof of causation in clinical negligence claims is different from scientific proof. Claims will ordinarily fail where the injury is likely to have been caused by one or more of a number of disparate factors, one of which being attributable to the defendant's negligence (see *Williams v The Bermuda Hospitals Board* [2016] UKPC 4; [2016] AC 888).

A material increase in risk is insufficient to establish causation (see *Gregg v Scott* [2005] 2 AC 176), although causation in some cases may be established on a balance of probability if the claimant proves that the breach of duty more than doubled the risk of injury (see *Sienkiewicz v Grief (UK) Ltd* [2011] UKSC 10). However, caution is required in stroke cases pursued on a doubling of the risk contention.

In the recent industrial disease claim of *Holmes v Poeton Holdings Limited* [2023] EWCA Civ 1377 the Court of Appeal was required to review the approach to causation and material contribution. The implications of the case will apply to stroke (and other clinical negligence) claims. A key takeaway was that the court held the material contribution principle/test (see *Bonnington Castings Ltd v Wardlaw* [1956] AC 613, [1956] 3 WLUK 6) applies to indivisible injury claims as well as matters arising from divisible injuries. The court highlighted that a risk factor is insufficient to prove material contribution in cases of indivisible injuries and there must be an established causative link.

A starting position is sometimes to appreciate that stroke is likely to be deemed an indivisible injury; which either it happens, or it does not. However, use of the word "indivisible" or "divisible" can potentially create confusion. Perhaps even more so in cases of alleged delay of giving thrombolysis treatment where the longer that thrombolysis is not administered, the more the severity of injury that can potentially arise.

Divisible diseases are those where the severity will be influenced by the total amount of the agent that caused the disease. Whereas indivisible diseases are those whose severity are not influenced by the total amount of the agent that caused it. Practically, applying the but for test within the case investigations can be more conducive and then going on to consider material contribution, if relevant.

The burden of proof remains on the claimant to establish "*generic*" and "*individual*" causation (addressed by Stuart-Smith LJ in *Holmes v Poeton*). When assessing causation, consider whether the alleged negligence of the defendant made a material contribution to the process which culminated in injury.

Across many clinical negligence claims, a claimant may place reliance upon *Bailey v Ministry of Defence* [2008] EWCA Civ 883; [2009] 1 WLR 1052 as the purported route to succeeding with a material contribution argument. *Holmes v Poeton* confirms that *Bailey* is authority for the principle that the material contribution test applies to indivisible injuries. Thus, *Bailey* is often the starting point as the key case for material contribution in clinical negligence. The claimant was successful in proving her case. Here, Waller LJ said:

> "*If the evidence demonstrates on a balance of probabilities that the injury would have occurred as a result of the non-tortious cause or causes in any event, the claimant will have failed to establish that the tortious cause contributed. Hotson exemplifies such a situation.*

> *If the evidence demonstrates that 'but for' the contribution of the tortious cause the injury would probably not have occurred, the claimant will (obviously) have discharged the burden. In a case where medical science cannot establish the probability that 'but for' an act of negligence the injury would not have happened but can establish that the contribution of the negligent cause was more than negligible, the 'but for' test is modified, and the claimant will succeed.*"

Waller LJ's reasoning on material contribution applies to divisible and non-divisible injuries but the use of "divisible" and "indivisible" are not referred to in the judgment. *Bailey* has been subject to some criticism but remains good law. In *Williams v The Bermuda Hospitals Board* the claimant succeeded using the application of material contribution. In this case, the defendant's negligent delay meant the single agent, sepsis, developed over approximately six hours progressively causing myocardial ischaemia. Lord Toulson stated:

> "*that process (sepsis) continued... longer than it should have done... on the balance of probabilities... the negligence materially contributed to the process, and therefore materially contributed to the injury.*"

However, Stuart-Smith LJ in *Holmes v Poeton* outlined that part of Lord Toulson's passage is "*liable to cause confusion and should not be adopted.*" The principle of material contribution is that the defendant should only be liable for the part of the claimant's ultimate damage to which they can be causally linked. Where a defendant is found to have caused or contributed to an indivisible injury, they will be fully liable for it, even if there may have been other contributing causes.

Holmes v Poeton confirms that material contribution applies to indivisible injuries and divisible injuries. However, practically, the principle remains complex. The contribution to damage from contribution to risk should be distinguished. Consider whether medical science can determine the 'but for' question and only if this cannot be answered, address whether medical science can establish that the negligent event(s) made a material contribution.

In *CNZ v Royal Bath Hospitals NHS Foundation Trust* [2023] EWHC 19 (KB) Ritchie J said in obiter:

> "*where the but for test cannot be satisfied due to scientific gap impossibility then the law will apply the material contribution to the injury test. If the claimant can prove the breach made a material contribution to the claimant's injury which was more than de minimis then damages are to be awarded against the defendant.*"

CNZ was essentially an informed consent (birth injury) case. Ritchie J held the defendant negligent for not offering the option of an elective caesarean. He concluded that the mother would have accepted this and that the cerebral palsy would have been avoided entirely as a result and applied the standard causation principles. However, he held that in the alternative, the negligence made a material contribution and as it was not possible to apportion between negligent and non-negligent caused ischaemia, even on that basis, the claimant would have been entitled to recover damages in full.

Material contribution can apply to stroke claims. It is necessary to establish the nature and extent of the injuries arise from the breach of duty and what would have occurred if no breach of duty had happened. Where a claimant suffers an indivisible injury, for which stroke would ordinarily be considered, if the injury was materially contributed to by the defendant, the defendant might be liable for the whole of the damage.

It remains a complex area and can sometimes be difficult in terms of proof. Most stroke cases will apply the 'but for' causation principles but when a stroke claim hinges on the material contribution test, it may depend on whether the defendant's breach contributed to the mechanism or process which caused the injury, as opposed to whether stroke is deemed indivisible. If a causative factor resulting from a breach can be regarded as having materially contributed to the outcome, despite it not being to be said that but for the breach the injury would likely have been avoided, causation can be established. Material contribution is (as Stuart-Smith LJ observes in *Holmes v Poeton*):

> "*an area that has been bedevilled by apparent inconsistency and imprecision at the highest level on multiple occasions.*"

Aetiology

Stroke is a heterogeneous condition with many variables. It can have several aetiologies and is multifactorial, as outlined in chapter one. When addressing causation, it will need to be explored and then addressed as clearly as possible within the medical evidence as to the aetiology of the stroke.

If the stroke has an array of potential causes which cannot be determined, then the principles in *Wilsher v Essex Area Health Authority* [1988] AC 1074 will likely minimise the chances of success for a claimant. If the defendant's negligence has merely added an additional risk factor that does not amount to a material contribution to the injury. See *Bell v Bedford Hospital* (in chapter one) and *AB v East Lancashire Hospitals* (in chapter four) as examples of multiple possible causes of stroke and causation was not/would not have been established in any event, if there had been breach. In *AB*, on the scientific evidence, the stroke could have been due to a "*huge range of other factors*" and in citing *Wilsher v Essex*, causation was not established.

In *ST v Maidstone* (referred to in the previous chapter), the breaches had not caused the damage and the claim failed on causation. The primary cause of the claimant's strokes was held to be a focal cerebral arteriopathy which was caused by the upper respiratory tract infection from which he was suffering. Such an infection was an established risk factor for arteriopathy and strokes in children. The claimant had (in the secondary claim) relied on *Bailey v MOD*, that the defendant's breaches of duty made a material contribution to the strokes but there was no objective evidence that the claimant's dehydration, acute-on-chronic haemolysis and severe anaemia contributed to the arteriopathy to cause his strokes.

It will be a fundamental part of the claim to establish the cause of stroke. If the court is not persuaded on the primary cause/aetiology because of many possible causes, then causation will probably fail.

Hypertension and atrial fibrillation (AF)

Treating hypertension adequately can lead to a decrease in the risk of stroke according to some evidence/literature available [The Lancet 2016]. Various papers and Handbooks conclude that with every 10mmHg reduction in systolic blood pressure, a significant reduction in the risk of stroke was observed. However, these studies do not demonstrate stroke would have been avoided on the balance of probability so they can be challenged.

AF increases the risk of ischaemic stroke. Some experts opine that anticoagulation reduces the risk of stroke by two thirds and others do not. Anti-coagulation should be given unless it is contraindicated but it can take some time for the agent to take effect. The length of time for anticoagulation to be 'effective' and whether its effects would have prevented stroke on the balance of probabilities can be a substantial point of dispute in stroke litigation. The expert evidence will need to carefully address causation.

Thrombolysis

Trying to establish that a claimant receiving thrombolysis following stroke would have prevented all damage occurring by applying the balance of probabilities test will be very challenging and this type of claim is unlikely to succeed.

If a non-negligent stroke occurs and it is alleged that thrombolysis would have improved the outcome for the claimant (if it was not given or given later than alleged in breach of duty) then this is an argument that might be pursued but causation is often disputed. The issue of whether the extent of damage is worse due to thrombolysis failures has literature weighted more favourably on the side of defendants but that does not necessarily mean a claim cannot succeed on causation. Each matter will need an individualised approach.

The research of Emberson J et al 2014 is often cited by defendants as the key literature that is alleged as unfavourable to a claimant. This is the analysis of randomised trials focusing on the effect of treatment delay, age and stroke severity. The paper concludes that alteplase (thrombolysis) significantly improved the overall odds of a good stroke outcome in patients included in the trials. However, the issue was that the benefits were limited to a proportion of less than 50% of the people.

In the Emberson paper, of those treated within three hours on symptom onset, around 10% did better with alteplase. In those treated between three and 4.5 hours after onset, 5% did better with thrombolysis. Those treated after 4.5 hours, 2% did better. Defendants often cite this publication demonstrates that less than 50% of people benefit from thrombolysis treatment to seek to defeat the balance of probabilities 'but for' test.

The main measure used to assess the benefit of thrombolysis in Emberson was the comparison of the numbers of people making a good recovery after alteplase compared with the number of people making a good recovery with control treatment. Defendants might argue that the appropriate measure is to compare the proportions of people who did badly without thrombolysis in the control group, compared to those who did badly with thrombolysis. This is not available in Emberson but is available in Lees et al 2010 which is another publication that a defendant may allege supports their position on causation. In Lees, more than half of the patients remained disabled three months after stroke despite thrombolysis.

The PRISMS trial by Khatri et al 2018 showed treatment with alteplase compared with aspirin did not increase the likelihood of favourable functional outcome at 90 days. Although the results were not considered conclusive, a defendant may refer to this as purportedly supportive literature. Further, Berge et al 2021 and Wardlaw et al 2014 concluded that thrombolysis does not lead to a more than 50% likelihood of reduction in disability from stroke at six months.

A claimant can consider the relevance of Tork et al 2020. This is a more recent (Egyptian) study that might be argued as favourable to a claimant. Here, a 'good' outcome occurred in 65.3% of patients versus a 'poor' outcome in 34.7% at three months. Hence, an argument using traditional causation 'but for' could apply. A claimant may allege that their previous health/condition was good (if it was) and an individualised assessment applies (particularly in young stroke) which gives better chances of a good outcome. However, defendants may seek to dismiss Tork, contending it was a single centre after thrombolysis with a low number of patients and not a study assessing the effectiveness of thrombolysis which requires large, multi-centred, double-blinded randomised studies.

Nevertheless, using statistics alone is just one strand of evidence as identified in *Marshall v Schembri* [2020] EWCA Civ 358. The Court of Appeal upheld the earlier decision of Stewart J in [2019] EWHC 283(QB) for a Fatal Accidents claim where the judge found that the admitted breach of the deceased's GP had caused the death as a result of pulmonary embolism. The issue was whether referral to hospital (by the negligent GP) would have led to thrombolysis or anticoagulation treatment which would have avoided death. The two available treatments would have been thrombolysis / heparin. It was held that the deceased would have survived. The court warned on the use of statistics alone and these are but one strand of evidence needed to prove causation. Although the precise mechanism of survival to the requisite standard could not be proven, the judge was satisfied that the result (death) that occurred was caused by the breach of duty.

A key observation is that each case should be reviewed as "*intensely fact-specific.*" The central issue in *Marshall* was, had the claimant demonstrated on the balance of probabilities that there were progressive pulmonary emboli and if so, would it have been picked up on monitoring had she been in hospital and if so, would thrombolysis have been prescribed and with what effect. Stewart J had looked at a study of the general effectiveness of thrombolysis and looking at matters in the round, it was held the deceased would have survived.

Antiplatelets and anticoagulants

Recurring themes within stroke causation are:

- Cases are 'fact-specific'.
- The available literature may not directly relate to the issues in a case.
- Claims are usually complex. Some claims will prevail and others will fail on issues that do not appear dissimilar at first sight.

Aspirin

Broadly, in some cases, having aspirin following TIA and non-disabling stroke can potentially work on the balance of probabilities at preventing new stroke events.

Expert medical opinion can often detail that aspirin needs more than 48 hours to take any effect on a person. Thereafter, it is arguable for its efficacy over the first seven days. After one week of aspirin (had it been prescribed), it might be possible to argue that it would more than likely have prevented the stroke. However, there can be arguments that there are no beneficial effects on the balance of probabilities after six weeks following administration for those in sinus rhythm and other conditions/situations.

If a claimant alleges that stroke would have been avoided had aspirin been given 48 hours or less prior to stroke, then this is primed for a causation dispute. If it is alleged that aspirin should have been given 48 hours or more prior to stroke, pending the circumstances, there is the possibility that stroke could be argued to have been avoided using 'but for' causation (if stroke occurs six weeks or less after aspirin should have started). If stroke occurs more than six weeks after aspirin should have begun, there can be arguments either way.

As evidenced by several unsuccessful cases, the effects of aspirin preventing stroke can be denied on causation. In *Owers & Anor v Medway* (mentioned in chapter two) the allegations surrounded failures to diagnose and treat stroke either by way of thrombolysis or, if not a candidate for thrombolysis, by aspirin. Whilst breach of duty was partially admitted for failing to prescribe the deceased aspirin after the stroke, causation was denied. It was held that causation was not established as that breach had not caused or materially contributed to the adverse outcome.

Furthermore, in *Watson v Lancashire Teaching Hospitals NHS Foundation Trust* [2022] EWHC 148 (QB) there was an alleged failure to diagnose TIA and prevent the claimant's major stroke through administering aspirin. Breach of duty was partially admitted, whilst causation was denied. Ritchie J held that the case failed on the facts. The earlier complaint by the claimant was more likely migraine than TIA. Moreover, even if TIA been established, the claimant would have failed to establish causation as it was held that aspirin would not have prevented stroke.

The Rothwell 2016 literature is often cited by parties in cases involving aspirin. The paper outlines that aspirin reduced the risk of recurrent stroke by around 60% during the first twelve weeks after TIA. However, Rothwell split up the 12-week period.

In *Watson*, experts agreed that Rothwell's general overall conclusion showed that aspirin reduces the risk of stroke after TIA in the patients included in the study. They agreed that that reduction was 60% overall (for all strokes, large and small) as stated in the paper. They also agreed the beneficial effects of aspirin occurred in the first twelve weeks and not thereafter.

Ritchie J applied the 'splitting' of the 12-week period when delivering the judgment. It was determined that there was no causation as the stroke occurred just over eight weeks after aspirin administration commenced and therefore applying Rothwell with forensic scrutiny, the claimant would have fallen into the 40% reduced risk band. Accordingly, the 'but for' test failed.

When analysing aspirin cases, practitioners should consider this 'splitting' element as Rothwell showed aspirin was effective in reducing the risk of all recurrent strokes (large and small) by 60% in the first six weeks and by 40% between weeks six and twelve. Therefore, it is important to apply the circumstances of each case to the minutia detail of the literature.

The Rothwell publication showed a risk reduction of more than 50% for patients with mild stroke and TIA treated with aspirin over the first six weeks. It also showed effects of over 50% in severe stroke for the first six weeks. It showed a reduction in stroke severity with the severest strokes being milder, although mild strokes were not cured. Experts may rely upon or criticise the Rothwell paper. Practitioners should test their expert on this paper if relevant and to avoid the potential 'trap' outlined in *Watson* by analysing the 'splitting-up' of the 12-week period. It is also likely necessary to consider age groups and the organic characteristics of the claimant.

The published studies suggest aspirin is more effective in preventing large vessel atherosclerotic stroke than other types (Rajkumar 2015). It might be seen that aspirin can provide high short term protection against secondary (second stroke) clotting but as not providing high protection against primary (first stroke) clotting, although this is a matter for medical science.

In *Choudhury v South Central Ambulance Service & Anor* [2015] EWHC 1311 (QB) the claimant suffered (a rare form of) acute ischaemic stroke causing 'Locked-in' syndrome. It was alleged there was a failure to act upon and treat recurrent stroke by giving aspirin. Breach of duty was partially admitted, whilst causation was denied. The Trust were found to be in breach but causation was not established, as that breach had not caused or materially contributed to a worse outcome. The available literature did not directly address the specific causation issue arising. The Rothwell paper was considered (although not as the primary literature) but the claimant was not suffering from TIA symptoms so this paper did not provide assistance. Cox J preferred the evidence of the defendant's stroke physician, finding that aspirin would not have improved the outcome. This case also sets out a helpful non-negligent chronology of events (at paragraph 34) that is illuminating for Ambulance Services and A&E breach of duty for managing acute stroke.

Treatment for child stroke typically involves aspirin or anticoagulation (usually if an embolic source is identified). The role of aspirin includes restoring or maintaining blood flow. In the acute phase of a stroke, the ischaemic core (the territory of the brain tissue deprived of blood supply) suffers damage whilst the surrounding penumbra (the part of the brain between the regions committed to die and those that receive enough blood) remains at risk. Aspirin can stabilise the penumbra by reducing thromboembolic occlusions. It also plays a vital role in reducing the risk of recurrent strokes.

Therefore, earlier initiation of aspirin in children has the potential to reduce the likelihood of further ischaemic insults. Studies (cited in RCPCH guidelines) suggest that early diagnosis and intervention are associated with better outcomes in paediatric stroke. Minimising delays in diagnosis/treatment correlates with improved functional outcomes. However, if a non-negligent ischaemic insult has already occurred, the extent of fast administration of aspirin improving the neurological outcome depends on the extent of the initial infarct, amongst other things. Causation can be particularly difficult in this type of case.

In paediatric stroke, aspirin therapy is primarily used to prevent further thromboembolic events by inhibiting platelet aggregation. There could be supportive evidence that aspirin therapy would have avoided stroke or improved the outcome for a child claimant. However, child stroke can present unique challenges in terms of diagnosis, treatment and outcomes.

Ischaemic stroke accounts for most child cases and this can be caused by a range of factors such as congenital heart disease, infections and genetic conditions. Children can experience stroke with atypical symptoms compared to adults. Clinically, the presentation is variable but often includes sudden hemiparesis, seizures, altered consciousness and speech/visual disturbances. Expert evidence will need to carefully address causation on the effects of aspirin.

Heparin

In some cases, heparin can be argued as a causative treatment agent to prevent stroke. Heparin works by interfering with the clotting mechanism in such a way that the clot stops growing; it does not operate to dissolve blood clots. When the clot stops growing, the fibrinolytic enzymes in the blood will slowly dissolve the clot and thereby gradually reduce the risk of part of the clot detaching. It might be argued that the risk reduces progressively the longer a claimant is anticoagulated.

Heparin is a strong anticoagulant and it can operate rapidly (within minutes of administration) and is supported by literature in this regard. Therefore, even claims that might appear to have an acute timescale of alleged/admitted earlier intervention, might still be able to be argued that 'but for' causation is applicable due to the ability of heparin to have an almost immediate impact.

In *Carter v Basildon and Thurrock University Hospitals NHS Foundation Trust* [2007] EWHC 1882 (QB) the failure to admit the deceased to hospital and treat her with heparin was deemed to be the cause of her death. Had the deceased, age twenty, been admitted when she should have been, on balance, she would have survived. She had given birth at the defendant's hospital and returned home the following day. Her baby was in a special care unit and she returned over the following days to visit. On the sixth day, at a post-natal check, she complained of headaches in the mornings but no action was taken. The next day she was too unwell to visit the hospital and remained at home. She then fell seriously ill and died in hospital the next day of cerebral venous sinus thrombosis. Breach of duty was admitted as she should have been admitted to hospital for assessment and observation after the post-natal check. Had she been, she would have been given heparin. The issue to determine was whether heparin, with other supportive treatment, would have arrested her condition so that she would not have suffered the fatal occlusion. She was deprived for approximately five to six hours of treatment and causation was established.

As noted earlier in *Pickering*, the claimant demonstrated they would have avoided the stroke due to the beneficial effects of heparin treatment which should have been given and continued until she was provided with anti-coagulation. The secondary clot formation would have been prevented.

There are of course circumstances when causation would not be established regarding heparin administration but if there were failings to provide heparin earlier/at all, then exploring causation is a worthwhile exercise.

Warfarin

Warfarin normally takes a few days to work fully. If a person stops taking warfarin, then their blood will usually start clotting as it did prior to its use after about one or two days. In *Thorley v Sandwell & West*

Birmingham Hospitals NHS Trust [2021] EWHC 2604 (QB) there was an alleged failure to resume warfarin treatment on timely basis (suspended whilst the claimant underwent coronary angiogram). Breach of duty and causation were denied and the claimant suffered an ischaemic stroke. The claim was dismissed. A reasonable body of experts would not have restarted warfarin treatment earlier and the claimant failed to establish that earlier resumption would have avoided their stroke. The secondary causation argument based on material contribution was also rejected.

As mentioned in chapter one, warfarin is usually the treatment of choice for AF. This is a condition that carries an increased risk of blood clots and consequent thromboembolic events including stroke. In consequence of unsynchronised atrial contraction there is a pooling of blood in the atria with a risk of formation of blood clots (thrombi). These thrombi can then break off and pass into the circulation (embolize) causing obstruction of a blood vessel elsewhere in the body (thromboembolism). When a blood vessel in the brain is blocked this can cause an ischaemic stroke, also known as a cerebrovascular accident (CVA). Warfarin / anticoagulation in people with AF can take a few weeks to be effective depending on the agent used.

As described in *Scott v Northern Devon* in the previous chapter, it was alleged the claimant would have been prescribed warfarin treatment to prevent the stroke. The claim was dismissed on breach but even with the limited time available, the stroke would not have been avoided so causation would have failed.

Other medicines

There are other groups of medicines that are prescribed to assist in reducing the risk of stroke and to help prevent vascular disease, as detailed in chapter one. In any case where it is alleged that medicine(s) / antibiotics / treatment would have prevented the stroke, a careful review of any relevant literature against the facts of the claim will be needed. In

McCabe, the claimant suffered a stroke secondary to infective endocarditis and causation was established as antibiotics would have halted the infection.

There are also medicines that are contraindicated in certain circumstances which can also give rise to a potential claim. For example, dalteparin is an anticoagulant used in the prevention and/or treatment of clot formation. It is routinely used to prevent DVT in legs for people immobilised in hospital. It should not be used in ischaemic stroke because of an increased risk of uncontrollable haemorrhage. If dalteparin is given to a claimant following ischaemic stroke allegedly causing haemorrhage, if breach of duty is established, then there is potential for causation. A large ischaemic stroke can result in haemorrhagic transformation but negligently being given an anticoagulant such as dalteparin can arguably cause haemorrhagic transformation. Therefore, when reviewing the use of medicines, check any contraindications in its use and if so, investigate whether that could have caused damage.

Consideration points

As indicated at the beginning of this chapter, stroke is likely an indivisible injury (see *Sims v MacLennan*) i.e. which either happens or it does not. The added complexity for some stroke claims is that a non-negligent stroke can occur followed by negligent treatment/management and/or followed by a negligent stroke. Distinguishing causation and damage can be complicated.

In *Sims*, an exception to the 'but for' test of causation was deemed inapplicable. The issue was whether the doctor's breach would have at least doubled the deceased's chances of having a stroke. It was accepted that there was a significant chance the deceased would not have had a stroke had he been treated for hypertension. At issue was the extent of that chance. On the evidence, it was not possible to find that the stroke was likely caused by a failure to treat earlier. It was not possible to say that it was probably not caused by a failure to treat. The best that could be said was that the breach increased the risk of stroke.

Manifestly, causation in stroke is a difficult issue. There is potential for future developments in this area. Material contribution can conceivably evolve further. Some concluding considerations are:

- Stroke is likely to be determined as an indivisible injury.
- The principles of material contribution set out in *Bonnington Castings* and in *Bailey v MOD* may apply to the claim but not necessarily.
- Causation disputes on the 'but for' test and material contribution are likely to remain in stroke litigation for the foreseeable future.
- Ensure the expert evidence addresses the aetiology of the stroke as far as is possible.
- Causation is often challenged/disputed in (non-negligent stroke) thrombolysis claims where the allegations concern thrombolysis improving the outcome. Current literature is more favourable to defendants but each case should be individualised.
- Cases alleging medication/drugs would have prevented the stroke are very fact specific. A careful review of literature is often needed.
- Literature on the specific issue is sometimes limited. Examine any available literature carefully.
- Causation is often complex in stroke litigation. Each case is unique and will require a bespoke analysis.

CHAPTER SIX

CONDITION, PROGNOSIS AND QUANTUM EXPERT EVIDENCE

This chapter sets out matters pertaining to collecting expert evidence in relation to condition, prognosis and quantum for a claimant following stroke. The following chapter (seven) then serves to dissect common themes and issues arising in these areas that usually impact quantum. The underpinning foundations explored are to assist in considering:

- What condition, prognosis and quantum expert evidence might be required in stroke claims.
- Case planning this expert evidence.
- Life expectancy.
- Obtaining a prognosis for all relevant conditions and issues.

<u>Proportionality (again)</u>

When considering the expert evidence required to address condition, prognosis and quantum, the need to apply the overriding principle of proportionality remains. The judge at a case management hearing will have this under constant consideration. Stroke cases are often inherently complex and extensive time and costs can inevitably be incurred through investigations and developing the evidence.

There is no rule that costs must be less than the damages achieved for the claimant but if costs are substantially higher than damages, the defendant might be more inclined to make submissions that aspects of the work performed was disproportionate. If this argument is raised by a defendant (it can still be alleged in high value stroke claims), then it would be prudent to have evidence surrounding the complexity of the matter to demonstrate that the work undertaken was reasonable and necessary. Nevertheless, it should be borne in mind that Lord Neuberger said obiter in *Ted Baker plc v Axa Insurance UK plc* [2014] EWHC 4178 (Comm) that:

> "*disproportionate costs, whether necessarily or reasonably incurred, should not be recoverable from the paying party. To put the point quite simply, necessity does not render costs proportionate.*"

However, recoverable costs can exceed damages but an analysis in this regard and on costs litigation is outside the scope of this book.

The overriding objective set out within the CPR Part 1 confirms the fundamental principle of dealing with a case at proportionate cost. Practitioners are required to help the court to further the overriding objective. If a claimant has suffered a stroke but quantum is likely to be limited to less than £25,000 – £50,000 (noting that there is no precision for what is arguably deemed as high value) then pragmatic solutions in respect of obtaining expert evidence to address prognosis and quantify a claim are needed.

This chapter addresses evidence on the basis of what might reasonably be required following a significant brain injury caused by stroke, with the caveat that each case will need a tailored approach. Despite some claimants suffering serious injuries, sometimes, various disciplines of expert evidence may not be permitted by a court, or a single joint expert may be ordered as opposed to a party obtaining their own expert evidence.

When life expectancy is predicted to be short, although Practice Direction 3D, Costs Management, provides for the court ordinarily disapplying costs budgeting when life expectancy is five years or less, the parties may be denied permission to obtain some reports that they seek.

In these circumstances, it will remain important to evidence matters in a fashion that still enables expert support for quantification issues. For example, if physiotherapy evidence is not obtained/permitted, then seeking the opinion of the neurologist, or rehabilitation medicine consultant, or care/OT expert to opine as far as they feasibly can on the claimant's physiotherapy needs would be a practical approach.

There is the prospect for joint instructions to expert(s) in stroke litigation. Although not a stroke case, in *Muyepa v Ministry of Defence* [2022] EWHC 2648 (QB) Cotter J proclaimed:

> "*the common working assumption (within higher value personal injury or clinical negligence claims)… that it is axiomatically the case that each party will have a care expert is misplaced.*"

The judge could be more willing to impose joint experts on parties, irrespective of the parties' submissions to the contrary. It will be worthwhile to assess whether any condition, prognosis and/or quantum experts can be instructed on a joint basis. This applies to all stroke cases irrespective of the value of the claim.

Expert disciplines

The common disciplines of condition, prognosis and quantum reports that may reasonably be needed in stroke litigation are:

- Neurologist/stroke physician
- Rehabilitation medicine consultant
- Neurosurgeon
- Neuropsychologist / neuropsychiatrist
- Neuro-ophthalmologist

- Urologist
- Physiotherapist
- Speech and language therapist
- Care
- Occupational therapist
- Accommodation
- Assistive technology

Other reports, such as cardiology, ENT surgery, and deputyship costs (and so on) may be required in certain cases. As in other personal injury and clinical negligence claims, the parties can make submissions in respect of any further Part 35 expert evidence they seek and this could include niche areas such as a pension loss report.

The medical evidence from the neurologist and/or rehabilitation consultant will usually be the leading disciplines for condition and prognosis. A neurosurgeon could be a key expert in haemorrhagic stroke. The same issues that arise in other neurological and brain injury claims relating to key features such as loss of earnings, care costs and accommodation claims are set out in far greater detail in other texts.

Expert evidence trajectory / the "roadmap"

Case planning is important in personal injury claims. When collecting expert evidence, it helps to review and determine the likely sequence of reports to obtain. Therefore, it may assist to prepare and keep under review a "roadmap" or plan of the expert evidence relating to condition, prognosis and quantum. This facilitates greater visibility on which experts may be needed and why, the timings of obtaining reports (so appointments can be scheduled in advance) and giving a clearer direction on progressing the claim. It will then also benefit ongoing communications with the claimant, defendant, case manager (if involved) and others because the plan/roadmap will indicate estimated timescales and provide greater transparency. It should also aid managing expectations of the claimant / their family in terms of the evidence needed and the proposed timeline in obtaining it. Keeping the evidence plan under review and updated will assist in giving focus and direction to drive the claim ahead.

Like dealing with cases of brain injury, usually, the leading discipline(s) of medical expert will prepare their reports first. The evidence should ideally develop organically whereby the sequence of reports are obtained giving clear opinion on condition and prognosis. This is not always possible and there will be numerous occasions whereby reports need to be sought "out of kilter" with the planned trajectory because events emerge. A common example is where the claimant is seeking to purchase a property due to the negligence and it may be necessary to obtain interim accommodation evidence on an urgent basis when medical evidence is awaited/incomplete. A flexible approach should be adopted in each case but it can be helpfully underpinned by an overarching case plan, or roadmap (or similar), of the expert evidence to obtain.

Life expectancy

A practical starting point, before developing a plan of expert evidence sought to be obtained, is to address the claimant's likely life expectancy. This does not necessarily mean to obtain a final expert opinion on the issue as the immediate need but to appreciate it being a feature of the claim. It will help with planning to assess whether there is likely to be a reduction to the claimant's life expectancy and whether it is likely to be a significant reduction. It is largely recognised and accepted by medical professionals (who treat and manage people with stroke) that people who have sustained a stroke will have a reduced life expectancy compared to the general population. If the stroke is particularly mild then a reduction in life expectancy might not be applicable but it will still be a point to deal with.

The approach adopted by the court to the assessment of life expectancy will be the application of multipliers used from the Ogden Tables, unless persuaded to the contrary. It is commonplace for life expectancy to be in dispute between the parties in stroke litigation. There are several matters worth considering regarding life expectancy before planning the expert evidence regarding prognosis and quantum. These include:

- What is the claimant's current age.
- How severe was their stroke.
- What domains have been impacted by their stroke; to include:
    - Communication (their ability to communicate problems for example);
    - Swallowing (are they at risk of aspiration [food or fluid can enter the lungs through the windpipe, which can cause pneumonia or a lung infection]);
    - Feeding (are they able to self-feed / are they PEG fed);
    - Continence (do they suffer from incontinence);
    - Epilepsy (do they have epilepsy);
    - Mobility (do they have mobility difficulties. If so, are they able to mobilise or are they confined to a wheelchair. What is their approximate tolerance for walking distance).

- Does the claimant have other health or medical issues that would potentially negatively impact their life expectancy. This could include things like:

    - A history of smoking; or excessive alcohol/drug consumption;

    - Obesity (a BMI [body mass index] of 30 or more);

    - Diabetes;

    - Cardiovascular disease; amongst other things.

It is beneficial to have a broad recognition of how life expectancy can be analysed/reductions that can apply in order to assist with case planning and other matters, such as preliminary quantum considerations and managing expectations. If a claimant has sustained a stroke and is over age eighty for example, based on the Ogden Tables, their remaining years of life are likely to be very few and proportionality will be important. Similarly, for claimants in their seventies, if various 'domains' are impacted (as outlined above) and/or they have prevalent pre-existing health issues, their remaining life expectancy may be particularly limited. Even if a claimant is relatively young, if they have suffered a severe brain injury and can no longer mobilise or self-feed (for example) then their life expectancy could be significantly reduced.

In most stroke cases, expert opinion will be required to set out the claimant's life expectancy. A standalone life expectancy report will not usually be required. However, as with other severe brain injury cases, a life expectancy report from a physician or statistician/actuary is a matter for consideration. If a life expectancy report is required, the same approach can often be adopted that is applied for other clinical negligence and personal injury claims. The parties will seek permission from the court to rely on expert evidence and pursuant to CPR Part 35, the court will control the evidence that is to be permitted. In *Dodds v Arif* [2019]

EWHC 1512 (QB) and cited with approval in *Chaplin v Pistol* [2020] EWHC 1543 (QB), Master Davison held that it is more convenient and cost effective for the clinical experts to give opinion on life expectancy. It was considered that standalone reports from a bespoke life expectancy expert should be confined to cases where the clinical experts cannot offer opinion, or they require specific input from a life expectancy expert.

Therefore, the starting point is ordinarily for a medical/clinical expert giving opinion on condition and prognosis to offer opinion on the claimant's life expectancy. Although a claimants' current age is no bar to expert evidence that may be reasonably required, generally, the neurologist/stroke physician and/or rehabilitation medicine consultant will be able to provide opinion on this issue. It can be a beneficial exercise to obtain life expectancy opinion from the neurologist/stroke physician expert and also a rehabilitation medicine expert, if the latter discipline is to be involved. Those experts can then be tested on their respective opinions.

The determination of life expectation in stroke litigation should be driven by the expert evidence in the particular case. Care should be taken to ensure that relevant literature is applied and an experienced medical expert gives opinion that is specific to the individual claimant. Stroke cases will frequently be likened to brain injury cases but there are limited literature studies of life expectancy following stroke with the features of many claims. It is important to also recognise that a loss or reduction in mobility can often be present following stroke and may deteriorate further over time. Therefore, the future trajectory and prognosis for a claimant's mobility will need to be understood and set out clearly in medical evidence because immobility can be a relevant factor to consider for its potential negative impact on life expectancy.

The main recognised research evidence usually cited when a serious brain injury has occurred is that of Brooks et al, Strauss and Shavelle. Brooks is the study that can be more commonly referenced and applied in stroke litigation but each case needs to be individualised. However, it is noteworthy that Brooks is based on traumatic brain injury (TBI), whereas stroke clinical negligence is not usually classified as 'traumatic' – rather, a non-traumatic or acquired (or similar) brain injury. Therefore, the application of the Brooks literature for stroke claims is not as relevant as it is compared to TBI.

Nevertheless, the available life expectancy literature for stroke is fairly limited in specific application so Brooks / Strauss / Shavelle (and sometimes others) are commonly applied by medical experts. Practitioners will benefit from being generally informed to this research and importantly, to bear in mind that it is based on studies in the USA and not the UK. The UK has better predicted outcomes for life expectancy than the USA for people that have suffered a brain injury, or not.

In *AB (by his Litigation Friend CD) -v- Royal Devon & Exeter NHS Foundation Trust* [2016] EWHC 1024 (QB), although this was a spinal cord injury case and the key issue determined was that illegality prevents recovery of Court of Protection costs by a claimant (during periods in which the claimant's incapacity was caused solely as a result of their illegal drug use, the doctrine of ex turpi causa should act to prevent the claimant from recovering damages in respect of Court of Protection expenses) Irwin J set out his conclusions in respect of assessing life expectancy. A critical analysis of the literature was explored and therefore, experts should refer to literature within their condition and prognosis reports, setting out how they formulated their conclusions. In *Royal Victoria Infirmary NHS Trust v B (A Child)* [2002] EWCA Civ 348 the Court of Appeal held that statistical evidence on life expectancy may be a useful starting point but it is wrong to decide life expectancy purely on the basis of statistics.

Cases which have considered life expectancy in cerebral palsy cases include *Whiten v St George's Healthcare NHS Trust* [2011] EWHC 2066 (QB) and *Robshaw v United Lincolnshire Hospitals NHS Trust* [2015] EWHC 923 (QB). The court relied on Strauss data. Having assessed the expert evidence, the first instance judges in *Whiten* and *Robshaw* adopted a three-stage approach, although not all experts will agree with this three-stage approach or methodology. Therefore, paediatric stroke claims may not follow the same approach but there is potential of its relevance and broad application. The 'headlines' for the approach used are:

- Stage one: Use US/Californian Strauss data to obtain the general life expectancy for a child of the age and disability of the claimant. Depending on their age, this can be done through Table III of Brooks 2014 or by a combination of Table II (table for life expectancy from age 4) and Table III (cohorts from the age of 15 upwards).

- Stage two: Uplift that general life expectancy to allow for the higher projected UK life expectancy figures.

- Stage three: After this, the specific features in the case are assessed to determine whether there should be any addition or reduction in that claimant's life expectancy.

A further point to review is that if a good care package is in place, then it should be explored whether this could lessen the reduction in life expectancy to be applied. In *Robshaw*, Foskett J added an additional two years of life expectancy for:

> "*the quality of the future care and the lifestyle*"

and declared:

> "*I do not see why the court cannot, in an individual case, seek to identify the risks that exist in an individual's life if he or she is a cerebral palsy patient and then consider the life that such a patient is likely to lead in the future and to determine how large those risks in truth are likely to be in that individual's life. In some cases, of course, the best care in the world may not obviate or materially reduce those risks. But there may be other cases in which it is quite plain that the risks to life are reduced by the quality of care to be received.*"

Robshaw cited *Owen v Brown* [2002] EWHC 1135 (QB) noting it factored the guidance given by the Court of Appeal in *The Royal Victoria Infirmary v. B (A Child)* as Silber J said:

> "....*I strongly agree...a significant positive factor that [was] correctly [taken] into account was and is the very high standard of care that the claimant receives and will receive. The effect of the award in this case is that the claimant will be the beneficiary of very high quality care in all the areas in which he requires it.*"

A similar approach was adopted in *Sarwar v Ali and the MIB* [2007] EWHC 274 (QB) and *Burton v Kingsbury* [2007] EWHC 2091 (QB).

If advising a claimant once expert opinion has been obtained, it can be a painful subject to discuss for them and forewarning them about the topic of life expectancy can go a long way. Some claimants do not want to read about it within an expert report. It can assist to inform the claimant/litigation friend in advance that opinion on life expectancy is to be given and to ascertain whether they want to be advised of it at that stage, or at a later date. If the claimant chooses to defer knowing about the life expectancy opinion, then the report can be provided to them in a fashion where it is not visible. There will come a stage when the claimant needs to be advised on this evidence and its implications but it may take a more staggered approach to help them process it.

Other texts can provide a resource in exploring issues with life expectancy in far greater depth. The takeaway points in respect of life expectancy for stroke cases are:

- Consider life expectancy from the outset to help with case planning.

- Stroke usually results in a reduction to life expectancy.

- Life expectancy can be argued as having a starting point as greater or lesser than the norm if evidence can be adduced in this regard.

- It can potentially be argued that life expectancy can be improved depending on matters such as quality professional care.

- The antithesis of the above is that it can be argued that life expectancy should be reduced further if various circumstances are present.

- The literature for life expectancy following stroke is not extensive. Having some background knowledge of the Brooks / Strauss / Shavelle papers can assist as a starting point.

- Obtain opinion from the neurologist/stroke physician.

- Obtain opinion from a rehabilitation consultant, if such a report is being obtained.

- Determine which expert(s) are the most suitable and appropriate to give the final opinion. Test the experts (usually in conference).

- The literature and statistics will be important but not the determining factor.

- A standalone life expectancy expert report is not ordinarily required but it might be in some circumstances.

- Be mindful of advising claimants / their family. Not every claimant wants to know the expert opinion in the report or conference and would prefer to be advised when the time suits them.

Obtain a prognosis

It is vital that a clear and detailed prognosis is given for the claimant's short, medium, and long term condition. It may be necessary for conference(s) with expert(s) to address issues relating to condition and prognosis.

A common feature following stroke, is the potential or likelihood of future deterioration in the claimant's condition. This can include issues such as:

- Mobility
- Functioning of limbs
- Fatigue
- Spasticity

In stroke cases where breach of duty and causation are admitted, getting access to interim funds is often a priority and it may be necessary for a claimant to undergo a period of rehabilitation before a final prognosis can be given. Meaningful gains could be made by a claimant with bespoke rehabilitation (looked at in chapter eight). Practitioners should draw out from the neurologist and rehabilitation consultant, what rehabilitation is likely required and when can a final prognosis be provided. As with other brain and neurological injuries, a final prognosis may not be able to be offered until after two years following stroke. There may also be the potential for delayed complications following stroke. These can include problems such as epilepsy and dementia so it is important that the medical experts set out the risk percentage, where possible, for the chances of future deterioration or development of complications.

Neurologist / stroke physician (or neurosurgeon)

This expert is often the expert to have reported on liability/causation, albeit not always the case. A neurosurgeon might report instead of a neurologist / stroke physician in cases of haemorrhagic stroke. Obtaining a report from this expert as the first condition and prognosis report is often a sensible beginning.

This expert (or a neurosurgeon) should address as far as possible, the claimant's neurological difficulties arising from the stroke and ensure they distinguish symptoms and outcomes that are due to the alleged negligent stroke, compared to symptoms and outcomes that would have occurred in any event. If the case is based on alleged delayed treatment (with better outcome) following a non-negligent stroke then the expert will need to make matters as clear as possible in comparing the prognosis against the condition/outcome that would have occurred anyway.

Subject to proportionality, this expert may then recommend a report from a consultant in rehabilitation medicine (see below). If that is not proportionate or recommended, then seek to ensure this report addresses all issues on the claimant's injuries and prognosis and any associated needs. The matters to address will range in each case.

The expert should confirm the spectrum of the claimant's condition as they age, should any deterioration be likely, or be at risk of occurring. Opinion on risks such as developing spasticity of muscles, developing epilepsy (if not present) (a neurosurgeon may need to defer to a neurologist on the epilepsy point) and future deterioration of mobility should be discussed and conclusions drawn. The expert may need to set out various matters such as how the stroke may impact employment, general accommodation needs (such as whether single level living is required), the impact on activities of daily living and a host of matters that would underpin quantum issues. There should be a clear vision of what difficulties they face now and what the future will hold for the claimant. It is often important to test this evidence and ensure that other experts have all the detail they need to provide their opinions.

Rehabilitation medicine

This expert will ordinarily use the report of the neurologist / neurosurgeon as the baseline for setting out their opinion. A defendant may contend in mild stroke cases, or those that are of low value, that this type of expert is not required. That will be an issue for each case. On the basis that it is reasonably required, this expert will address more bespoke issues to include the multi-disciplinary rehabilitation regime needed in the short and long term. They may detail the input required for rehabilitation, the duration of rehabilitation and interventions that may be necessary. They may detail supportive comments or direction for other matters such as equipment, care, transport, accommodation requirements and such like.

A rehabilitation medicine expert may have more experience of treating patients following stroke in the long term because if a stroke patient is treated by a neurologist, any long term follow-up is largely on an ad-hoc basis. As outlined earlier, this expert might deliver the leading, or only, opinion on life expectancy. Any contradictions or inconsistencies between this expert and the neurologist should be addressed and the evidence should be made clear.

Neuropsychologist / neuropsychiatrist

It is more likely that a neuropsychologist expert is required to report on the claimant's potential neuropsychological difficulties, possible change of personality and other cognitive issues following stroke; as opposed to a neuropsychiatrist. The latter expert may be more relevant if the claimant already had pre-existing psychiatric issues prior to their stroke. Like other brain injury cases in personal injury and clinical negligence, whichever discipline is instructed (despite them being distinct) should report on the extent of the brain injury, its impact, any treatment needs and give a clear prognosis. Sometimes both disciplines will prepare a report but this is less common.

Stroke can cause injury to the brain causing a range of cognitive impairments and neuropsychological deficits. Texts focussing on brain injury describe matters in more detail surrounding points like intellectual and executive functioning, memory loss and psychological functioning. Depression is a common feature of stroke, particularly in young patients. Approximately 30% suffer depression. The expert will likely need to perform a number of neuropsychological tests (such as the Test of Premorbid Functioning, the Wechsler Adult Intelligence Scale, the Boston Naming Test and so on).

A practical point to consider is ensuring that any tests performed by different neuropsychologists are sufficiently separated in time because tests performed in too close proximity together can invalidate the results. For example, if the defendant's and claimant's respective experts wish to examine the claimant less than six months apart. Seek input from the expert(s) should this point arise.

The report should set out in detail the condition of the claimant's cognition such as:

- Memory;
- Concentration and focus;
- Multitasking;
- Communication;
- Information processing;
- Cognitive fatigue;
- Planning and organising;
- Mood and emotions;

- Behaviour;
- Personality; and
- Capacity.

It will assist the expert to have the two aforementioned expert reports available to them, along with any lay witness statements that detail issues for the claimant, including matters outlined in the above bullet points. In finalising this expert evidence, the assessment of performance and validity / effort will need to be understood to ensure there was no deliberate underperformance by the claimant.

The expert should usually set out the claimant's pre-stroke intellectual abilities compared to their current level and give a final prognosis where possible. Sometimes a re-examination after treatment sessions is required. The expert should opine on how any difficulties will impact upon their daily functioning and activities of daily living such as undertaking employment and self-care.

Neuro-ophthalmologist

If the claimant has suffered visual dysfunction/disturbance following stroke, a neuro-ophthalmologist report may be required. Neuro-ophthalmology merges the disciplines of ophthalmology and neurology focussing on the interaction between the brain, nerves and eyes. As the eye is connected to the brain by the optic nerve, it carries signals from the retina to the brain which are then interpreted as visual images.

Blindness and other serious ophthalmic problems can arise following stroke. The extent of visual loss should be determined as it could factor into other areas such as their need for care and equipment/technology. The claimant may benefit from rehabilitation and care that is focussed on the visually impaired. It is important to check with the claimant or their family for any complaints of visual disturbance and for the neurologist or rehabilitation consultant to comment on this and give opinion on whether an ophthalmic report should be obtained.

Urologist

A urologist specialises in diseases of the bladder, kidneys, prostate and male reproductive organs. They can diagnose, assess and treat conditions like incontinence which can arise due to stroke. The muscles and nerves of the urinary system work together to hold and release urine at the correct time. Nerves carry messages between the bladder, spinal cord and brain which tells the bladder muscles to tighten or release. Damage to the brain from stroke can disrupt the normal voiding of urine as the nerves and central nervous system are impacted.

Ensure the medical records are carefully reviewed and progressively updated to check for any complaints relating to incontinence. If the claimant has incontinence following (a negligent) stroke and did not have it previously, an expert urology report may be required. Urological issues are delved into further in the next chapter.

Physiotherapist

If the claimant has physical dysfunction due to stroke and it is recommended by the medical expert(s) for them to have physiotherapy and for a specialist report to be commissioned, then an expert report may be required. A physiotherapy report will be less common in cases where quantum is more limited. In those cases, it may be that the neurologist / rehabilitation consultant / care/OT expert sets out the recommended future physiotherapy regime and costs as far as possible, in order to address quantification for the physiotherapy head of loss. However, those experts are not specialists in this discipline and where the claimant has suffered significant neurological injuries from stroke, physiotherapy is often one of the core essentials of rehabilitation. Lifelong maintenance to try and avoid or reduce long term complications such as contractions arising could be required.

If a physiotherapy report is obtained, the expert may set out the aims of treatment such as maximising physical and functional abilities, treating potential secondary musculoskeletal problems and trying to reduce tone. They may recommend a goal orientated physiotherapy programme and detail other matters like equipment needs, orthotics, carer training (for example, for an exercise regime), along with hydrotherapy, having a personal trainer and gym attendance. The expert should detail the costs for all recommendations and the reasons for such.

Speech and language therapist

A speech and language therapist (SaLT) report may be required if the claimant has communication difficulties following stroke. The report should set out the short, medium and long term speech and language therapy needs and associated costs. They should explain the extent of the difficulties with communication and language and what is the likely prognosis.

Sometimes there can be overlapping issues for the SaLT and neuropsychologist experts to address. It assists for these experts to see the report of the other expert discipline before finalising their respective opinions. Similarly, it can benefit to have all experts able to see all the available reports before they are disclosed (if this is possible).

The SaLT will likely perform tests and assessments with the claimant. There can be a range of tests and these can include, for example, the Test of Reception of Grammar (TROG) and the Mt Wilga High Level Language Test. The expert may also address swallowing problems (if in existence) but they may need to defer to an ENT surgeon if it is especially complex. Similar to obtaining a physiotherapy report, it is a specialist discipline and is often needed in high value claims but when proportionality is a key issue, it may be that other solutions need to be considered to help quantify the costs of any potential SaLT regime.

Care and Occupational Therapist

As with most personal injury cases, care and occupational therapy report(s) often attract the most potential in respect of quantum for the case. The future (and past) cost of care, case management and equipment/OT/transport/other related needs can be substantial when a claimant is seriously injured from negligent stroke. One of the preliminary decisions will be whether to instruct one expert to cover both issues or to have two experts, with a nurse reporting on care and the occupational therapist reporting on OT and equipment needs. This will be case specific but proportionality will need to be considered.

Stroke cases are no different from other clinical negligence claims in respect of what type of report(s) to obtain in this regard. The care/OT expert(s) evidence will usually be crucial when neurological/brain injury has occurred from stroke and can provide substantial impetus regarding quantum. Each case should be considered for the potential need for such evidence.

Accommodation

Whether an accommodation report is required will depend on each case but if the claimant has suffered from serious injuries following stroke, it is often the position that their current accommodation is likely to be unsuitable to meet their needs. They may require level access accommodation, carer space, storage for equipment, an area for therapies and so on. As in other personal injury claims, a review of whether a report is needed should be undertaken, especially when life expectancy is limited.

For stroke (and other) claims, there can be situations arising when a claimant has, for example, a ten-year life expectancy remaining and their accommodation is considered by other experts to be inadequate to meet their needs and often unsafe. Consideration will be needed for the approach to adopt for any potential accommodation head of loss. If a report is obtained, then the expert would likely need all the available reports as outlined above and would set out the options, their recommendations and associated costs.

Assistive technology

In serious and catastrophic injury (high value) stroke cases, an assistive technology report may be required. That is not to say that this evidence is excluded in cases of low or moderate value, but that it is more commonly only obtained when the claimant has suffered significant injuries that may require them to need/benefit from specialist technology. The expert could have a variety of backgrounds (before becoming an Assistive Technology expert) such as:

- An electronic or software engineer;
- A clinical scientist;
- An occupational therapist.

If a claimant has sustained injuries from their stroke such as becoming blind, or a wheelchair user (at the time of assessment or in the future), or having limb dysfunction by way of examples, they may benefit from various items of technology and environmental controls. Expert evidence would need to address what items they would benefit from, the reasons behind that, the costs of any such items/technology/equipment, the replacement timescales and associated expenditure such as installation fees, maintenance support and professional advice. Items of equipment and environmental controls can range from things such as laptops and mobile phones to door openers and curtains/blinds openers.

If a joint report is obtained, this does not mean that the parties are bound by the recommendations set out in the report. For example, the defendant could still contend that the equipment will not be used by the claimant, or that it is not reasonably needed. This expert report is often obtained as one of the final reports because the technologist will likely need to have the medical evidence, along with the care, occupational therapy and accommodation (and potentially other) evidence available to them to provide opinion.

Deputyship costs

If the claimant is a protected party or child and there is a Deputy, or proposed Deputy, then an expert report may be required to set out the costs of having a professional Deputy for as long as needed in the particular case. If, for example, it is a child that will have capacity to manage their finances at age 18, then the costs may cease at that age. The expert will set out any one-off or similar costs, such as winding up fees, and the annual costs of the Deputy being required. This expert will also be one of the final (if not usually the final) reports to obtain in the sequence of condition, prognosis and quantum evidence collection. The expert should be provided with all the available evidence and they may need to have various information such as the likely amounts for the heads of loss in the Schedule of Loss (if the Schedule has not yet been prepared), any incurred Deputy fees, the court orders with the assessment costs, whether the claimant has a will, and any potential risk of the will being contested.

Summary of condition, prognosis and quantum expert evidence

The key summary issues are:

- Keep proportionality in mind when determining the evidence required.

- Consider whether any joint instruction(s) to experts are suitable.

- Consider life expectancy early on and address this when planning evidence collection. Remain sensitive to the claimant and their family when giving advice.

- The leading opinion for condition and prognosis will usually be the neurologist/stroke physician or neurosurgeon and/or rehabilitation medicine consultant.

- Consider developing an expert evidence roadmap / case plan for the condition, prognosis and quantum reports to obtain.

- Keep the evidence/case plan contemporaneous and adjust it where needed. Include the claimant in the trajectory planning.

- Ensure a clear prognosis is given which includes the spectrum for potential or likely deterioration of the claimant's condition as they age.

- Get the expert evidence clear and the rationales carefully explained within the reports. Seek experts to consider alternative scenarios where suitable and to set out the outcomes on the claimant's case and where possible, on the defendant's case.

CHAPTER SEVEN

COMMON KEY ISSUES IN STROKE CASES UNDERPINNING QUANTUM

This chapter seeks to outline in more minutia, some of the more prevalent key issues that are ultimately related to quantum that can arise in stroke cases and to identify points for review. As ever, each case would require its own tailored set of explorations and clarifications. The focus here is on the groundworks required to help tackle some of the issues feeding into quantum that inherently arise in stroke litigation.

Quantum judgments

There are not many recent full quantum judgments available for high value brain injury claims arising from stroke. It is important that when utilising another case as a comparator, that any relevant heads of loss are adequately uplifted to be contemporaneous and that each case is decided on its own merits.

A recent large loss quantum judgment was delivered by Ritchie J in a birth injury case, *CCC (a child proceeding by her mother and Litigation Friend MMM v Sheffield Teaching Hospitals NHS Trust* [2023] EWHC 1770 (KB). Although it is not a stroke case, a number of the issues determined by the judge can be applicable to quantum in stroke claims. Of further interest, at the time of writing, judgment is awaited from the Supreme Court in respect of whether the claimant is entitled to "lost years" earnings from the defendant.

Nearly all the claimant's experts were preferred to that of the defendant which laid the foundations to a seemingly excellent outcome across all heads of loss for the claimant (also pending the Supreme Court decision for "lost years"). Ritchie J skilfully sets out the general principles in the determination of quantum for heads of loss and the judgment is an invaluable read. The current key outcomes from *CCC* [2023] that could potentially be applicable in high value stroke claims includes:

- No deduction was applied to the sum for past gratuitous care.
- Two waking night carers were permitted.
- A home hydro pool was allowed.
- Guiding commentary from the judge on the principles regarding quantum issues.

The extent of the claimants' disability

As described in the introductory section of this book, a stroke can range significantly in how mild or severe injuries arising from it can be. In each case, there will need to be an understanding of the extent of the claimants' disability to assist with quantification issues. A preliminary task will often be to obtain medical expert opinion on whether the claimant is classified as disabled due to the stroke. This will impact matters including the application of multipliers from the Ogden Tables in respect of future loss of earnings. If there is no loss of earnings claim to be presented, if the claimant had already retired for example, then it can still assist to clarify the extent of their disability. This enables a greater understanding of the claimant's all-round needs which will be relevant to quantum experts such as care, occupational therapy and accommodation.

Ensuring the medical report(s) give opinion on whether the claimant meets the criteria for being defined as disabled is therefore a matter to consider. It should be clarified that any such disability arises from the (negligent) stroke and confirms whether they were already disabled, or would have become so, from a non-negligent condition. The leading legislation to address this is set out within the Disability Discrimination Act 1995 and Equality Act 2010. Importantly, within the Ogden Tables, the former Act is distinguished from the latter in that the Ogden definition requires the claimant to be disabled under the more restrictive 1995 Act and for the disability to affect either the type or amount of work the claimant can do.

The medical experts, most likely in the disciplines of neurology/stroke physician, rehabilitation medicine and neuropsychology (and perhaps others like neurosurgeon / neuro-ophthalmology) should give opinion on the extent of the claimant's neurological and neuropsychological (and any other) injuries. It can assist for the medical experts to describe the brain injury in terms akin to mild, moderate, moderately severe, severe, or similar language. The extent of the disability from stroke will then feed into the myriad of issues and play a fundamental role in underpinning the heads of loss and items claimed.

The extent to which a claimant is disabled and the impact it has upon them can be a common point of dispute in stroke litigation. If appropriate, well-prepared agendas for the medical experts and joint statements can help to narrow issues, albeit to factor in the points described in chapter three. Witness statements can supplement the expert evidence to illustrate how the stroke impacts their activities of daily living. When drafting the Schedule of Loss, care should be taken with accurately and effectively describing the claimant's disabilities to give a powerful narrative surrounding the losses presented.

Functionality

Similar to addressing the extent of disability, the ability of a claimant to function to their maximum potential following stroke is often an issue to explore and clarify. There can be an abundance of challenges faced with how they may be functioning and the evidence should specify matters in detail. To better understand a claimant's functionality following stroke, the following issues (amongst others) can be considered:

- Incontinence
- Mobility
- Neurological difficulties
- Spasticity
- Neuropsychological deficits
- Epilepsy
- Communication and language
- Fatigue

The concept of functioning is broad and each claimant will differ. Some will have similar conditions with those managing adequately despite their difficulties, whereas there will be others that struggle to function because of the problem(s) they face. It is useful to discuss and examine any difficulties in detail with the claimant and witnesses to evidence how they manage, or struggle to manage, with the particular features they have. Some of these issues are set out in more scope below to help unravel potential disputes that can arise that would impact quantum and consequent points to consider.

<u>Incontinence</u>

Urinary incontinence is the inability to control urine leaving the bladder. A stroke can cause urinary incontinence to develop and a report from a urologist may be required. Sometimes, incontinence is not an immediate problem but it develops progressively over time. It is important to keep obtaining updated medical records and seeking updates surrounding the claimant's condition and any developments as the claim progresses.

There are various types of bladder difficulties such as:

- Urge incontinence – the feeling of a sudden, urgent, uncontrollable need to pass urine.
- Frequency – needing to urinate more often than usual.
- Nocturia – waking from sleep with an urgent need to urinate.
- Nocturnal enuresis – wetting the bed whilst asleep.
- Overflow incontinence – bladder leakage when it is too full. This occurs when a person has lost feeling in their bladder so they cannot recognise when it is full and the need to pass urine.
- Reflex incontinence – urinating without knowing it.
- Stress incontinence – dribbling urine when coughing, laughing, sneezing.

Bowel problems can also occur, including faecal incontinence. This is usually only when the stroke has caused a severe brain injury. Conversely, constipation can sometimes arise which might be caused by a combination of using additional, or certain types of medication, and impaired mobility meaning the claimant is less active. Being less active can contribute to constipation.

Disputed quantum issues that can arise (and are worth reflecting upon to prepare in advance of such prospect) in respect of urological dysfunction include:

- Are any urological/similar investigations required and if so, what are they, and what are the costs.

- How much, if any, input is needed from a urologist in the long term for consultations and reviews.

- Are any aids and equipment needed such as pads, catheters and toiletries.

- Is surgery needed or likely needed in future.

- Are Botulinum Toxin injections (otherwise known as Botox) required into the bladder and if so, what is:

  - the likelihood of success;

  - the cost of each course of treatment;

  - the frequency of treatment required;

  - the impact of successful Botox injections upon episodes of incontinence.

Various investigations for the bladder may be necessary such as:

- Ultrasound scan – to investigate a potential range of issues e.g. kidney stones, incontinence, UTIs, bladder emptying.

- CT scan – to check function / signs of disease.

- Cystometry – to assess bladder function.

- Video Urodynamic Studies – to show what happens to the lower urinary tract when it is filling and emptying.

The above issues regarding incontinence can create a range of disputed points that are rooted into quantum. Often, a claimant may not be able to access the aforementioned investigations and treatment options on the

NHS but sometimes they may be able to. The defendant may contend that reviews and treatments will be performed on the NHS. This argument usually has reasonable prospects of being defeated if the claimant is unable to access this input on the NHS and is shown to be utilising privately funded input (if available to them). Further, there is the supportive legislation of the Law Reform (Personal Injuries) Act 1948. This confirms there shall be disregarded the possibility of avoiding expenses by utilising NHS facilities.

If it is agreed that the claimant requires urology input on a private basis, then the next points of contention are usually the frequency and costs of such input. Expert evidence will likely be required but if the claimant is having input during the claim, then the costs being incurred can be utilised as evidence in support of what may be needed in the future. It might assist to also calculate the annual average based on incurred costs if future ongoing input is likely at around the same level.

Botulinum Toxin injections are usually the most expensive aspect of long term urological difficulties if they are performed on a private basis. Annual costs can run into thousands of pounds. The cost of surgery may be the highest one-off cost as sometimes procedure(s) may be recommended such as fitting a suprapubic catheter. Incontinence can be a very disabling issue and if the claimant suffers with this due to negligent stroke, it can become a head of loss that has numerous disputed issues within it. Practitioners should stay vigilant to investigating urological dysfunction.

Mobility and neurological difficulties

Mobility and neurological problems have been grouped together in this sub-section for ease of discussion but they can be distinguished in stroke claims as separate difficulties as the claimant might have satisfactory mobility but suffer neurological problems affecting their upper limb(s). People that have suffered from stroke may have sustained neurological damage causing their muscles to not work like they did before. This can cause problems like weakness, paralysis, contractures, spasticity and various other complications.

Unfortunately, there is often permanent damage caused following stroke. Reduction in the claimant's mobility is a very common feature. After stroke, if there is paralysis, this usually occurs on one side of the body. If the stroke occurs in the left side of the brain, the right side of the body is affected and vice versa. Nevertheless, stroke can affect both sides of the body, usually if it occurs in the brain stem. If one whole side of the body is paralysed, this is called hemiplegia. It differs from hemiparesis which is partial weakness/paralysis. For example, weakness in an arm or leg. Weakness can vary in severity, from mild, where it mildly affects one part of the body to severe, where it affects the whole side of the body.

Mobility

Neurological damage can sometimes cause a claimant to rely upon a wheelchair (whether ad-hoc/all the time) or to need walking aid(s). One of the key aspects to explore (which can be a point of dispute) is whether the claimant's condition will likely deteriorate in the future to render them becoming a full-time or part-time wheelchair user if they do not currently need a wheelchair. To dissect this further will often include determining issues such as:

- Is it likely the claimant will become reliant upon a wheelchair for ambulation.
- If so, at what age.
- Are there any stepped changes during this development. For example, will the claimant progressively deteriorate due to the stroke causing them to need a wheelchair outdoors at a certain age and to then need one indoors at a later age.

The extent of the claimant's mobility dysfunction can be a point that needs addressing in detail. Especially in younger stroke where future deterioration is a risk but the claimant might still be able to walk unaided, albeit with limitations such as:

- Struggling on inclines / with difficult terrains / or anything other than a level surface.
- Using stairs.
- Distance they can mobilise without needing to stop to rest.

Matters to clarify (that can frequently be disputed) will often include issues like:

- Is a walking stick required indoors/outdoors.
- Is a wheelchair required indoors/outdoors.
- What is the prognosis for walking/mobilising ability. The claimant's evidence may project that they will become wheelchair bound at a future age due to deterioration in their condition. A defendant might challenge this opinion and contend this will never materialise, or that it will at a later age than alleged.

Due to stroke, it might be contended by a claimant that the effects of ageing can be superimposed on them and more pronounced at an earlier age. The main thrust surrounding this is whether it would result in the claimant having increased care, equipment and other needs in future. This could be an issue of contention and the medical experts would need to address this. A stepped regime may be postulated, whereby the claimant alleges they need a certain amount of care up to a particular age and it then increases further. If the claimant is young, there could be a number of incremental increases in the amount of care, case management and other needs arising should the medical evidence detail that their condition will progressively worsen with age. Sometimes, a claim for future alternative accommodation is sought to begin at a certain age due to projected deterioration in mobility and function from neurological weakness/problems.

Mobility can be negatively impacted progressively by various other difficulties such as hip joint abnormalities and spinal/postural problems from over-use of one side and poor gait. It is important to ascertain how the claimant's mobility will be in the long term and this can be a common feature that is in dispute.

Another layer in respect of immobility is that should a claimant be/become a wheelchair user, they may have a risk of developing pressure sores from prolonged sitting which can become an added complication. Expert opinion may be required to address the chances of the development of pressures sores occurring and how that would then link into any additional needs if one arose.

Transferring

Another key issue that can significantly impact quantum arising from neurological deficits caused by stroke is the ability to transfer. Whilst a claimant may currently be able to independently transfer on and off things like the toilet, sofa, bed, chairs, into their car and so on, as they age, transferring can sometimes become more difficult, painful and an activity/task that requires another person(s) for support. It may be that they are already struggling or unable to transfer independently since their stroke.

It will be necessary to obtain medical expert opinion on whether the claimant will be able to transfer in the long term. Furthermore, to ascertain the potential for any shoulder/hand/other damage arising from over-use of the upper limbs from transferring / being a wheelchair user.

With increased tone and spasms, with one or both sided weakness and impaired control, this could impact their ability to perform transfers independently, as well as fatigue. The ability to independently turn in bed can also be a contentious issue because if the claimant is unable to turn over when asleep due to weakness, they may allege that more night care is needed to turn them which could increase the costs of any recommended night care regime.

Various contested issues can arise in relation to transferring such as the need/extent of care and equipment. For example, with care, it may affect the amount of care needed because if a claimant cannot transfer on/off things, it may be alleged that their care needs require extensive support to ensure a carer is available to help them manage their toileting/other needs which are unpredictable. Another issue to clarify will be whether it is safe for one carer to help the claimant with transferring or if two persons are required.

Equipment needs would need addressing as a claimant may require hoisting and this could result in things like a mobile hoist being required and ceiling track hoists set up in their home. Transport needs may be impacted if there is an inability to transfer as a specialist wheelchair accessible vehicle may be contended as needed.

The equipment and costs for mobility related losses will heavily depend on the care/occupational therapist expert evidence. The expert(s) should set out their analysis of why the claimant reasonably requires care/support/items and whether the claimant would have required it in any event or at some point in the future. The claimant's (in)ability to transfer can be a crucial part of a stroke claim in respect of quantum and careful consideration should be given to this. The inability to transfer can have a notable impact on quantum.

Spasticity

Spasticity can arise due to stroke. This is the constant contraction of a muscle. As the brain has been damaged by the stroke, the signals sent by the brain to muscles may be disrupted and not co-ordinated, causing the signals to tell the muscle to contract all the time. With time and the ageing process, muscles affected by spasticity can become tight, stiff, painful and less functional. Measures to assist with reducing or preventing spasticity are important for a range of reasons to include maximising the independence of a claimant and limiting pain.

Evidence should set out the likelihood of spasticity remaining / increasing / worsening as the claimant ages, or alternatively, improving with good management. Linked to this is whether the claimant has already had any treatment for spasticity, whether on the NHS or a private basis and what benefits, if any, were seen. This can assist the medical experts to give a prognosis for spasticity.

The main treatment for spasticity is Botulinum Toxin injections and the drug, Baclofen. Other medications sometimes used are Dantrolene, Tizanidine, Diazepam, and Phenol Blocks. Botulinum Toxin injections are usually injected directly into the muscles that are affected from the stroke. The costs and the frequency of such treatment(s) on a private basis can be a point of dispute so evidencing the need and benefits from use can assist. There may also be gains if the claimant were to undergo therapies such as physiotherapy and hydrotherapy.

Some of the issues that can arise in stroke litigation regarding spasticity include:

- The ability of the claimant to perform activities of daily living.

- Their employment prospects, if any.

- Pain management.

- Treatment/therapy costs and frequency.

Physiotherapy, hydrotherapy and orthotics

Spasticity and other difficulties can result in physiotherapy and hydrotherapy being contended as needed. The extent of physiotherapy treatment/input and associated costs are often areas of dispute in stroke litigation (and other claims). In any personal injury case, hydrotherapy can be a big issue between the parties. The more contentious aspect is usually the cost of claiming a hydrotherapy pool at home. This can be expensive and it can be challenging to recover the costs of this. Nevertheless, in *CCC* there was a detailed review by Ritchie J in respect of the hydrotherapy pool at home claim and it was awarded in that case. It is apposite to consider this case when pursuing this head of loss in appropriate claims.

If the claimant has mobility difficulties then orthotics may be recommended. Input from an orthotist, along with an occupational therapist and physiotherapist may be necessary. It is unlikely that a Part 35 expert report on orthotics is needed but the expert evidence should address any needs surrounding orthotics. The physiotherapy expert can usually deal with orthotics in their evidence.

<u>Neuropsychological deficits</u>

In respect of quantum issues arising from neuropsychological deficits, the key aspects are divided here (in a very broad manner) as twofold, by way of an overarching explanation. Firstly, the costs and amount of treatment/therapy needs that arise from neuropsychological deficits. Secondly, addressing how any cognitive impairments are connected to other heads of loss and how the deficits may shape a claimant's needs.

In respect of the former point, the main thrust of quantum issues will include things like:

- Neuropsychology treatment costs (hourly rates).
- The number of sessions required.
- Any contingencies such as sessions for set-backs and emergencies.
- Any other recommended treatments such as clinical psychology / psychosexual therapy / interaction with SaLT and general input required.

In respect of the latter, much broader aspect, which is usually a more fundamental issue, will be the presence and extent of interconnected neuropsychological difficulties arising from stroke. The issues arising can be extensive, such as the impact on employment, care, equipment/technology, general damages and so on. The claimant's capacity can be a key disputed matter between the parties if the claimant's evidence is that they lack capacity, whereas the defendant's evidence is that they retain capacity. This can create disputes in numerous matters including the need for a professional Deputy and the associated costs of such, the extent of care, the claimant's earnings ability and so on. Practically, testing the expert (and potentially the claimant pending the circumstances) in conference may be a requisite exercise.

Epilepsy and Provisional Damages

Stroke can cause epilepsy. It can be evident after the stroke or, as mentioned in the previous chapter, it can be a delayed complication that subsequently arises. Epilepsy can be a very disabling condition. An important issue for practitioners will be to ascertain expert evidence, likely from the neurologist, on whether the claimant:

- Now suffers from epilepsy due to the stroke; or
- Would have had epilepsy in any event; or

- Now has a risk of suffering from epilepsy in the future due to stroke and if so, what is the percentage risk attached to this.

A starting point can be to consider, 'what is epilepsy' because it is not always agreed/straightforward that the claimant has epilepsy. The definition of epilepsy is arguably somewhat ambiguous. Differing authorities describe it and there does not appear to be an agreed definition. The NHS describes it as a common condition that affects the brain and causes frequent seizures. However, the International League Against Epilepsy, The World Health Organisation, and the International Bureau for Epilepsy do not all have the same definitions.

Stroke causes scarring of the tissue in the brain which results in brain damage. The structural damage in the brain results in disordered electrical activity which can become chaotic, causing seizures. There is literature that suggests a 3% – 67% risk of seizures occurring several years post-stroke (Xu MY, Stroke & Vasc Neurol 2019). The literature varies and some indicates the risk of seizures as the risk could be 11.5% within five years following a large ischaemic stroke (Postgrad Med J. 2006; 82; 568-572). The type/extent of stroke usually impacts the risk of seizures.

There can be disputes on whether the claimant is classified as having epilepsy. Consequently, there should be confirmation of whether they have epilepsy within the medical report(s). Otherwise, this poses the prospect of the defendant disputing the existence of epilepsy and the medical evidence being silent on this point.

If the expert neurologist identifies that the claimant now suffers from epilepsy due to the negligent stroke, or has a risk of suffering from epilepsy in their lifetime due to negligent stroke, some further matters to consider will be:

- Can their seizures be managed with medication.

- If not, what is the likely management plan for them.

- What is the risk of their epilepsy becoming refractory.

Should seizures become an issue, a claimant is likely to require further MRI brain imaging and further EEGs. Long term follow-up from a neurologist may be necessary. The costs of neuro-imaging and follow-up may be argued if epilepsy is due to the negligence. Seizures will most likely be controlled by anti-epileptic medication but not always. Some further quantum issues that may arise if epilepsy is established due to stroke negligence include:

- General damages. Whether epilepsy increases the amount for pain, suffering and loss of amenity. There is scope that it does in certain cases, even when the brain injury is already significant. The disabling effects of epilepsy may cause the claimant to suffer from additional fatigue and periods of hospitalisation for example.

- Life expectancy. Whether this is reduced further due to the presence of epilepsy.

- Special damages. Some example heads of loss that can be impacted include:

    - loss of earnings;

    - care and case management;

    - Therapies and treatment;

    - Transport.

In respect of special damages, it may not necessarily be the epilepsy that causes any change to the amount of loss to be claimed/recovered, as a claimant may already have a significant brain injury that renders them incapable of undertaking remunerated employment for example.

However, in relevant cases, it should be considered whether epilepsy increases a claimant's needs. For example, if they have seizures and require two support workers to be available when outside the home for the event a seizure occurs, as opposed to only one support worker being required. This could have a dramatic effect on the cost of care claimed/recovered. Another example is that current DVLA rules would likely prevent them from driving for at least 12 months since their last seizure. This may then impact the transport/travel head of loss. Further investigations could then include, whether any extra costs are likely to be incurred for somebody needing to drive the claimant, or, for example, the claimant's need to take taxis instead of driving themself.

Those representing claimants should be sharp to the future risk of epilepsy occurring if this is linked to the stroke and to clarify that the risk would not be there absent any negligence. Should there be a material risk, then Provisional Damages may need to be pleaded/claimed. Practice Direction 41A CPR deals with Provisional Damages. When considering the opinion of the medical expert (neurologist/stroke physician) in relation to any potential future risk of epilepsy, if purportedly due to the stroke, it will assist to clarify the percentage chances of epilepsy occurring and to ascertain the chances of epilepsy becoming refractory if it does materialise.

Inevitably, there will be cases where the claimant has non-negligent epilepsy, or the risk of epilepsy was present in any event, or where there is not a requirement for Provisional Damages. If the claimant is not at a material risk of serious deterioration in their condition then this award may not be suitable. The medical evidence should be teased out on these issues.

Communication / language / speech difficulties

Stroke can cause speech, language and communication deficits. These can include:

- Dysphasia. This is impairment in the production of speech. It is also known as aphasia. It is a disorder that affects the ability to communicate verbally. It varies in its severity. There can be difficulties with talking, understanding others when they talk (even though hearing is unaffected), reading written words, writing, using numbers and performing calculations.

- Dysphagia. This is a swallowing disorder.

- Dysarthria. This is a motor speech disorder that makes it difficult to form and pronounce words. When speaking, the speech may be unclear, making it difficult for others to understand what has been said. Speech can be slurred or slow.

The above can all be present together. Communication difficulties may also intertwine with neuropsychological / cognitive dysfunction. Common issues that arise in stroke litigation in this area include:

- The extent of speech and language difficulties.

- The cost of private speech and language treatment sessions.

- The total number of treatment sessions that may be required in the short to long term.

- Management of communications through use of technology / equipment.

- The impact of communication difficulties in respect of matters such as potential employment and care needs.

It is important to recognise that a claimant may retain capacity and yet have severe communication difficulties. Practical support may be required for the claimant such as pacing when giving them information/advice and applying the most suitable method(s) of communication. The evidence will need to address matters. Being mindful of proportionality, it may be that, for example, the claimant would benefit from face-to-face visits when appropriate, especially if video conferencing is difficult for them.

The claimant may need to give oral evidence at trial, which whilst uncommon, is still a possibility. Practice Direction 1A CPR addresses vulnerability of parties or witnesses which includes communication or language difficulties amongst other things. This should be considered for the claimant, or indeed any party participating in proceedings and/or giving evidence as special measures can be put in place.

Fatigue

Fatigue is a common problem, occurring in around 30% of people following stroke. The impact of fatigue is subjective and a key issue is sometimes the extent and impact of fatigue on a claimant's activities of daily living, care needs and employment prospects. Witness evidence may be a crucial element of describing the effects of fatigue on the claimant. Further, the case manager (or experts/practitioners) might recommend the claimant and their family keep a fatigue diary. This diary would set out how tiredness and fatigue impacts their day/night over a period of time. Such a diary can, if appropriate, be shared with Part 35 experts and disclosed as part of standard disclosure. Any care records should also (ideally) detail fatigue. Various other documents obtained as part of disclosure, such as employment records or DWP records, should be reviewed to note references to fatigue as part of the review.

The impact of fatigue can increase with age. This can be a contested issue and the medical experts would need to address the prognosis for fatigue and how it interplays with activities of daily living as the claimant ages. Management of fatigue may require input from an occupational therapist and supervision from a case manager, should this support be available to a claimant. If fatigue is present, then it is necessary to be cognizant to the claimant's needs when communicating with them in order that they can adequately manage their fatigue.

Summary

A plethora of issues will commonly arise in stroke claims creating the potential for substantial disputed points relating to the claimant's outlook/prognosis/needs and ultimately being associated with contested elements on quantum. Matters feeding into the expert evidence and ultimately, the Schedule of Loss and Counter Schedule can be extensively disputed. Invariably, the central themes often surround the heads of loss that are likely to attract the highest damages in the particular case, along with life expectancy.

For instance, general damages, loss of earnings, care and case management, accommodation, therapies/treatments, equipment and transport amongst others. There can be much debate on all heads of loss. It is important to put in place the scaffolding surrounding the finalised evidence and to recognise issues that might need to be tackled in advance of settling a Schedule of Loss and proceeding towards Alternative Dispute Resolution (ADR). To re-cap some of the key elements underpinning issues relating to quantum:

- Address the extent of the claimant's disability. Are they classified as disabled. How will this impact loss of earnings and/or other heads of loss.

- Ascertain their functionality in light of any deficits/difficulties the claimant has.

- Check and review at intervals whether a change in the claimant's condition is present (such as incontinence developing). If it is, further work to address that will be required.

- Ensure the medical evidence is transparent on the spectrum for the short, medium and long term prognosis of all aspects of the claimant's condition.

- The medical evidence should be nailed down so that any mobility, neurological difficulties and other deficits are clearly mapped out to include any deterioration and stepped changes.

- Investigate the prognosis for transferring ability and other potentially delayed complications.

- Deal with any issues surrounding epilepsy and Provisional Damages. If epilepsy is present, make this clear. If there is a risk of it developing, set this out and whether it would lead to a serious deterioration in the claimant's condition if it materialised.

- Consider whether any communication and fatigue problems require adjustments for the claimant and do not underestimate the potential significance of the effects of these.

- Each claimant is unique and every case will have its own distinct issues. Where proportionate, meticulously addressing matters such as those posited above will help develop solid foundations for when the inevitable disputes occur.

CHAPTER EIGHT

STROKE REHABILITATION

Following a Letter of Response, if a full admission of liability has been made by the defendant(s) then subject to the wishes and instructions of the claimant, it should provide the opportunity for interim payments to be obtained. This can enable a claimant to undergo a tailored rehabilitation regime, should this likely be of benefit to them. The extent and requirements of rehabilitation will depend on numerous factors for each claimant such as the severity and damage caused by the stroke, the available support, and their goals.

Initial rehabilitation challenges in clinical negligence

One of the most frustrating aspects of stroke (and other clinical negligence) litigation for practitioners, and of course for many claimants, is the inability to obtain privately funded rehabilitation until an admission on breach of duty and causation is obtained. Any such admissions are unlikely to be achieved within 18 months of the initial instructions to investigate a potential claim. It can often be years before admissions are given and frequently, no admission is ever received and private funding is unavailable during a claim. The Rehabilitation Code 2015 applies to personal injury claims and does not extend to clinical negligence, despite it being widely accepted that early intervention rehabilitation is instrumental for maximising long term recovery benefits. For stroke survivors, the optimal window for the most effective rehabilitation to occur is usually firmly closed.

Unless a claimant can self-fund initially following stroke, their reliance is usually on the NHS to provide their rehabilitation. The resources available on the NHS are arguably incomparable to private treatment and thus, there is often an inability for a claimant to optimise their post-stroke condition. One of the further concerns with this obstacle is that the best opportunity to try and maximise gains occurs within the first two years following stroke. Consequently, the best outcomes may never be achievable and rehabilitation may need to be more extensive due to the delayed commencement of a suitable regime.

Following stroke, a claimant may have spent weeks, months, or even over a year in hospital. Thereafter, sometimes they reside in a residential rehabilitation unit. They may then have been discharged home, or to an alternative home if their residence was so unsuitable that it would be impossible for them to live there. They may need to go to a care home (or similar) depending on the level of severity of their brain injury and neurological difficulties. Housing and care needs are two crucial concerns for a claimant and their family following a serious stroke and without access to adequate funding, many lead exceptionally difficult lives.

There is a marked distinction for stroke claims compared to brain injury claims arising from other forms of personal injury, such as road traffic accidents, in that interim payments are not provided by the NHS (NHS Resolution) until negligence is admitted. Even then, interim payments may not be forthcoming or timely. Managing the claimant and their family's expectations is needed. This can be challenging.

Life following stroke can be dysfunctional and completely disrupt the claimant's personal and family life. The added stress and potential fatigue of litigation can sometimes weigh heavy on their shoulders so managing the claimant, and sometimes their family, is an integral part of the claims process. This can sometimes intensify once the opportunity to step away from the NHS regime into the private sector becomes available as there is an urgency to get specialist rehabilitation proceeding.

The statutory therapeutic input provided in respect of rehabilitation is usually limited to a handful (or less) of things like:

- Physiotherapy;

- Occupational therapy;
- Speech and language therapy;
- Psychological / neuropsychological input;
- Intervention/treatment such as Botox injections;
- Some basic equipment being provided.

It can perhaps be described as a "postcode lottery" in terms of the therapeutic input provided following stroke. There may be people who have benefitted from many therapy sessions on the NHS but this is not commonplace in the author's experience.

Interim payments

If liability has been admitted to the extent that is sufficient for interim payment(s) to be requested, then obtaining interim monies should ordinarily be at the forefront of matters when representing a claimant following stroke. Subject to interims being agreed and promptly provided, then progress with rehabilitation can usually occur. If the claimant is a protected party or child, then Rule 21.10 CPR applies in that any voluntary interim payment will require the approval of the court. An application to court will then be required.

A Deputy may also be appointed to manage the monies. Practically, if the claimant lacks capacity and a Deputy is to become involved then notify the Deputy as soon as possible of the admissions. It helps to give a proposed Deputy advanced notice of the matter and the expected date the Letter of Response is due to enable the Deputy to set up a pending file should they choose to do so.

The potential Deputy will often visit the claimant to explain their proposed role before they are instructed by the litigation friend. This might be an opportunity for practitioners to also visit the claimant to assist in explaining the process and possible avenues for progress and rehabilitation if an admission is received.

A reasonable sum to request for an interim payment will depend on each case and consideration should be given to the amount of monies to seek for the claimant. For a rehabilitation programme to get started with the implementation undertaken by a case manager and multi-disciplinary team (profiled below) then adequate funds to support this will be needed. Funds will likely need to be ample enough to cover at least a number of months of rehabilitation.

Estimated projections of anticipated costs should be gathered by the case manager, usually within an Immediate Needs Assessment (INA) report. If there is a Deputy involved, they will usually also provide estimated projections of expenditure once information is gathered. Both these estimates will assist to plan ahead and forecast the timing and amount of further interim payment requests.

When requesting an interim payment, this should (where possible) be done promptly. It could be at least another four weeks (and often longer) to receive a response from the defendant as to whether the interim is agreed (in full, or in part). Thereafter, it may take several more weeks for the monies to arrive. The claimant may be eager to launch into rehabilitation and having monies readily available could be of paramount importance to them.

Keeping an open dialogue of good communication between all relevant people is essential in respect of interim payment planning and requests. Ongoing reviews are required to avoid the claimant risking exhausting their interim monies and disrupting a rehabilitation regime. It is good practice to keep the defendant regularly updated and given sufficient notice and plans surrounding interim monies and further/future requests.

Stroke rehabilitation goal setting

A conceptual analysis of stroke rehabilitation is a process of active change by which a claimant who has become disabled acquires the knowledge and skills needed for optimal physical, psychological and social function. The service element could be considered as using all means to minimise the impact of their disabling condition and assisting them to achieve their desired level of autonomy and participation in the community/society.

Having an overarching goal is recognised as an important feature in stroke rehabilitation. A goal is a future 'state' that is desired and/or expected. The 'state' might be relative changes, or an absolute achievement. As part of the goal, setting smaller goals is also essential. This is the process of the claimant agreeing on goals with their respective rehabilitation team and others around them. There is evidence to show in post-stroke rehabilitation that:

- Goal setting is associated with more behavioural change.
- Setting both short term and long term goals is more effective.
- Changes are more likely if goal setting is supported by specific intervention.

The latter point is poignant as those who have suffered stroke require interventions and if the rehabilitation options are unsatisfactory, then optimisation of recovery is unlikely to be achieved. A claimant can still make significant functional gains, even around five to ten years after their stroke. Therefore, in any clinical negligence stroke case, where there is an option for bespoke rehabilitation to occur, the evidence/literature indicates that this can help a claimant and it should be considered.

The literature reviews indicate that a claimant must play an active role in rehabilitation if improvement is to occur. If they are suffering from psychological and/or neuropsychological difficulties that impede their engagement, then steps may need to be taken to address these matters first, before a more comprehensive regime can be put in place. The research shows statistically significant improvements for activities of daily living and functional outcome parameters with rehabilitation following stroke. The claimant's goals and the goal setting process that is performed by any privately funded case manager and rehabilitation team should be kept under ongoing review and monitoring.

Rehabilitation as a 24-hour process

The British Society of Rehabilitation Medicine sets out standards for rehabilitation services. These standards include:

- Rehabilitation being a 24-hour process.

- All major decision-making meetings e.g. assessment, goal planning, conferences, and discharge planning should be undertaken by the inter-disciplinary team, in conjunction with the individual, and their family and carers where appropriate.

- The individual and/or their family should be provided with appropriate, accessible and timely information to allow them to make/participate in decisions regarding their treatment and care.

- The person should participate as actively as possible in agreeing and reviewing their rehabilitation goals, which should include long and short term goals.

When reviewing the rehabilitation recommendations for a claimant, it is important to remember that the claimant is at the heart of the process and it is their objectives that should be strived to be achieved. Promoting a rehabilitation regime may be required alongside advice on the potential recovery of expenditure that is being, or to be, incurred. It is an all-encompassing structure to provide the claimant with necessary scaffolding and support to help maximise their independence and function after stroke.

Case management

Whether case management proceeds by using interim monies will ultimately be a matter for each individual, alongside the reasonable need for this cost arising due to stroke. It is not a pre-requisite that a claimant should instruct a case manager and undergo rehabilitation in a stroke case before a claim can be settled. Without access to monies this is not feasible. A claimant in their later years of life (for example) may wish to advance their claim by progressing towards settlement opportunities / Alternative Dispute Resolution at the earliest juncture. Some may not wish for a case manager as they may feel their needs are not enough to justify it, or that they want to manage things independently.

Case management is detailed in many other texts but is worthy of a brief mention here. Claimants should be advised of the potential benefits of case management (ideally already supported by Part 35 expert(s) if possible). Should this be an option, then identifying a suitable case manager would be a key initial task for rehabilitation to begin. Practitioners should be proactive in this process.

Obtaining several CVs of case managers that reside within a sufficiently close geographical location to the claimant, with experience and specialism in brain / neurological injury / stroke should be sought. Ideally, they would be part of BABICM (British Association of Brain Injury and Complex Case Management). It is important to review the CVs of case managers and explore their experience and credentials to ensure they are equipped to deal with the claimant's needs. It can be a good idea to send the CVs to the claimant for consideration and to discuss potential preferences to thereafter invite to interview.

A "meet and greet" event is a staple part of introducing a potential case manager to a claimant and their family. This can otherwise be known as a "beauty parade" whereby a few, usually two or three, case managers are introduced to discuss matters and the claimant would choose their preferred person after some reflection. A case manager is then often instructed to act by the claimant's practitioner on a unilateral basis (that is the instructions only come via the claimant and not as a joint exercise with the defendant).

An INA report is prepared by the case manager and this will set out the initial recommendations and costs for the short term; usually in the region of six to twelve months. The case manager's duty is to the claimant, as confirmed in *Wright v Sullivan* [2005] EWCA Civ 656.

Practitioners should endeavour to develop a good rapport with the case manager. This will be more advantageous to a claimant as there will often be much communication between the claimant, case manager and legal representative. The case manager can be changed if so required. Subject to a case manager being needed, they often remain an integral part of organising and co-ordinating rehabilitation, care, and many other things for the claimant during the claim and beyond.

A multi-disciplinary team

Where required, the case manager may create and co-ordinate a multi-disciplinary team (MDT) to provide therapies and review the claimant. The team will often consist of some/all of the following disciplines:

- Neuro-rehabilitation consultant
- Neuro-physiotherapist
- Occupational therapist
- Neuropsychologist / psychologist
- Speech and language therapist
- Orthotist
- Assistive technology consultant

- Music therapist
- Educational psychologist for children
- Vocational therapist

In addition, there could be other medical investigations required. Input could be necessary from a neurologist to consider issues like epilepsy/seizures, an ENT surgeon for serious swallowing concerns, a neuro-ophthalmologist for investigations into sight/vision and so on. The case manager is usually tasked with building a tailored team to suit the needs of the claimant.

In stroke cases, always staying vigilant and conscious of the claimant's non-negligent condition and prognosis is needed to be able to advise the claimant on the likely recoverability of costs of rehabilitation and expenditure. For example, if the admission on breach of duty and causation is limited to the claimant's stroke being more profound and deemed that they would have still been left with some dysfunction (neurological and/or neuropsychological, or other) then it will be important to distinguish within the expert evidence, what rehabilitation would have been needed in any event, despite the negligence. Those costs may not be recoverable within the claim if causation as to condition is in issue.

Claimant practitioners will benefit from attending the MDT meetings. Valuable discussions and points can be explored during these meetings. The costs element of doing so is recoverable in principle, confirmed in *Hadley v Przybylo* [2024] EWCA Civ 250 which is the lead case on the recovery of costs for lawyers attending rehabilitation meetings.

It may be necessary to obtain the privately funded rehabilitation records from the MDT members and case manager. There are several reasons for this including:

- The records will shed further light on the claimant's needs, difficulties, progress and goals.

- The records might assist to evidence improvements with functioning achieved during rehabilitation.

- They may contain information or details that would otherwise not have been communicated, such as difficulties for the claimant completing specific tasks.

- Records will form part of disclosure and would need to be sent to the defendant.

- The Part 35 experts will usually benefit from reviewing these records to finalise their reports/evidence.

The rehabilitation records will need to be carefully reviewed before they are disclosed to the defendant. Some records might be identified as deemed "litigation privileged" and not for disclosure. For example, the claimant's legal representative providing legal advice within correspondence contained within the records that has been shared with the case manager or a member of the MDT.

The MDT members should prepare reports. There is usually an initial assessment report and then quarterly reports so there is an up-to-date summary of matters. Some claims will differ. The MDT reports are to summarise the rehabilitation, goals, progress, recommendations and costs, amongst other things. The reports should be considered with the claimant and case manager and they will be disclosed to the defendants as the claim progresses. It helps to keep an ongoing index and bundle of these reports. Ongoing liaison with the case manager in conjunction with the claimant will be needed. The MDT reports will ultimately be disclosed to the defendant and provided to the Part 35 experts to review them for preparing/updating their expert reports.

Residential or community-based rehabilitation

One of the preliminary considerations for the claimant might be to determine whether rehabilitation is best suited for them via a residential package or undertaken in their home and local community. It will often be necessary to have expert opinion from a rehabilitation consultant (the Part 35 expert and/or the treating consultant within the MDT) to opine on what programme may be most effective to the claimant and to endorse any plans and costs.

Sometimes, residential rehabilitation is deemed suitable in the beginning to "kick-start" an intense programme of input. This could include a number of weeks spent at a specialist facility. They often have overnight accommodation if the claimant is not based locally. There are a few of these specialist facilities across the country and although they are funded on a private basis, there still could be delays in waiting for a space to become available. The costs vary and a quote should be obtained, usually by the case manager, or the claimant. The defendant should be informed of the plans surrounding this by way of courtesy and good communication. After a residential package, a claimant may then opt to continue rehabilitation in their local community.

Alternatively, a community-based rehabilitation regime may be developed from the outset. This is where the claimant would undergo sessions of treatment, either at local clinics, in their home, or sometimes a combination of both. This is the more common scenario compared to residential rehabilitation.

Care/support

An important task for the case manager might be to create a care package for the claimant. It will need to be made clear if the claimant would have required any care but for the negligence, and if so, to what extent. There may be significant legal arguments in respect of the claimant's pre-existing or non-negligent condition, or the claimant being put to proof as to the extent of their injury. The medical and care experts will need to provide adequate detail surrounding this which can be a difficult and in-depth investigation. Even when the claimant had no care needs prior to stroke, the costs and extent of care is usually a hotly contested issue.

The cases of *Sklair* and *Reaney* may be relevant to some claims. In *Sklair v Haycock* [2009] EWHC 3328 the claimant was able to recover his care costs (a 24/7 commercial care package) in full which arose from his negligently acquired spinal cord injury, with no deductions for his pre-existing Aspergers syndrome and OCD because the care he would now need was qualitatively different. It was different in kind compared to his pre-existing condition.

Conversely, in *Reaney v University Hospital of North Staffordshire NHS Trust* [2015] EWCA Civ 119 the defendants were only liable for the claimant's increased care needs. It was held that if a defendant's negligence causes care and other needs which are substantially of the same kind as the claimant's pre-existing needs, then the defendant is not liable for those unless they are qualitatively different.

The key issue in this setting is whether the care needed is qualitatively different and each case will be assessed on its own issues. Additional care could be either:

- Quantitively different – where the defendant is responsible for the difference;

- Qualitatively different – where the defendant is responsible for all the care.

For claimants that have suffered stroke due to negligence and the stroke itself would have been avoided and they had no pre-existing care/conditions, this issue will be of less relevance but can nevertheless still be subject to challenge and arguments. If they had pre-existing conditions causing some care to be needed (or likely needed in future), then a *Sklair* argument might be available to the claimant to contend that the quality of care now needed from the stroke was different. However, *Reaney* could apply which could limit the amount to be recovered. It will be case specific.

The case of *Martin v Salford Royal NHS Foundation Trust* [2021] EWHC 3058 is worthwhile considering as the claimant was awarded the full cost of private care and not just the additional care needed due to her significant brain and neurological injuries. Like various other cases, stroke claims can have the quantitively versus qualitatively analysis applied in the assessment of causation as to care needs.

On a practical point, if a case manager is developing a care regime, the claimant and case manager (and Deputy if involved) will need to be carefully advised, based on expert evidence, as to what is potentially recoverable and/or at risk of challenge. Ultimately, if by the time of approaching trial a claimant has a care package in place that is the proposed 'full' regime required for them and it is evidenced as working well, this can be powerful in persuading a trial judge what is needed long term.

Rehabilitation synopsis

- Rehabilitation is an integral part of promoting and trying to maximise the independence of a claimant following stroke.

- In suitable cases, seek to obtain interim payments as soon as possible should admissions on breach of duty and causation be received.

- For claimants that are governed by CPR Part 21, inform the proposed Deputy in a prompt manner if there is an admission and/or interim funds are being sought. Obtain approval of interim payments from the court for these claimants.

- Goal setting forms part of the heart of rehabilitation. Keep the claimant's goals and objectives under review and maintain good communication in this regard.

- Advise the claimant on case management if interim monies are available. If the claimant wants a case manager, then organise this instruction.

- Obtain and analyse all rehabilitation reports and records. Some records will need to be identified as privileged and potentially redacted for disclosure to the defendant if attracting litigation privilege.

- After careful review, provide disclosure of therapy reports to the defendant at suitable junctures.

- Consider and explore the rehabilitation recommendations of the case manager, MDT members and rehabilitation consultant. Seek to obtain further interim monies where possible if they are required.

- It is the claimant's case. Encouragement, support and advice should be provided through their journey but ultimately, it is the claimant's decision as to whether they want to engage in rehabilitation; recruit a case manager, MDT and support workers and so on.

CHAPTER NINE

SETTLEMENT

This topic encapsulates general aspects of settlement that may arise in stroke cases, although much will apply to other claims. It is not a forensic analysis of the components of settlement such as Part 36 offers, but a sweeping narrative on practical matters enveloping settlement.

Most stroke cases will not reach trial. They are either compromised by settlement or claimants do not continue their claim due to insufficient prospects of success. An assumption is made that the claim is well founded and the defendant(s) are willing to engage in dispute resolution. A snapshot of common practical issues to consider are succinctly enumerated below.

Apply the basic principles

In the tort of personal injury, a claimant is entitled to reasonable compensation but not overcompensation to put them back in the position they would have been in if they were not injured, so far as money can achieve this, but for the negligence. Full compensation should be provided. Lord Blackburn in *Livingstone v Reynolds Coal Company* [1890] 5 AC 25 set out principles for the courts to apply in assessing quantum. Beginning the analytical process of settlement preparations with the basic principles can assist even when dealing with complex, high value stroke claims.

In *Manna v Central Manchester University Hospitals NHS Trust Foundation* [2015] EWHC 2279 (QB) Cox J quoted Lord Woolf in *Heil v Rankin* [2001] 2 QB 272 that a claimant:

> *"is therefore entitled to damages to meet his reasonable needs arising from his injuries. Reasonableness always depends on the particular circumstances and it applies to the head of loss claimed and to its amount."*

The courts have addressed the principles of compensation in many cases and applying those principles to each stroke case will help facilitate a greater understanding of the likely range of compensation awards that could be achieved at a quantum trial. This will help in terms of settlement planning, advising and negotiating. The evaluation of legal principles could be set out in extensive depth and is briefly mentioned here to merely emphasise the importance of keeping the basic principles of compensation in mind when dealing with settlement considerations.

Settlement goals

Like other clinical negligence claims, the overarching outcome in stroke litigation is to conclude a claim. Navigating a successful resolution for a claimant in a stroke claim adopts the same fundamental issues surrounding settlement of a claim across the clinical negligence landscape. Much will depend on a variety of issues such as the goals and instructions provided by the claimant / defendants, liability, causation and quantum.

Preparing the claim thoroughly will help underpin the ability to achieve the goals for the claim but acting expeditiously is also necessary. Settlement is not always simply to try and 'maximise' damages if acting for a claimant. It is important to ascertain the claimant's goals and drive the claim ahead using these as the guide. A claimant may have their goal as achieving the fastest settlement possible so it is necessary in each stroke claim to confirm the settlement goals.

<u>Proportionality as a continuum</u>

There are many forms of negotiation that occur in clinical negligence cases. Engaging in ADR requires ongoing consideration of proportionality. The value of the case will usually impact the determination of how the forum for negotiations may occur. The quicker that parties can reach the point in time to negotiate a potential settlement, the better it will normally be for the claimant and more likely to reduce overall costs.

In low/modest value claims, a balance is to be struck in focussing efforts on a case to be able to effectively engage in ADR without having turned over every single stone, but having a strong degree of clarity in the strengths and weaknesses of the case.

If the claim is pleaded for hundreds of thousands or multi-million pounds then it is more likely that a Round Table Meeting / Joint Settlement Meeting (RTM / JSM) will be required, or in some cases, Mediation. Whereas if the case is claimed in the tens of thousands of pounds, then without prejudice telephone / video call or written offers / Part 36 offers (or similar) are more likely to be used as the avenue for negotiations.

ADR focussed telephone and video discussions between the legal representatives are becoming more commonplace which is a positive step. This can enable more flexibility and help build relationships with opponents so 'battleground' issues can be tackled more directly. This can limit the propensity for becoming entrenched in protracted written communication 'warfare'. The parties are encouraged to engage in all forms of ADR and indeed, court directions make this clear. As in other clinical negligence cases, offers of settlement and negotiations in stroke claims can take place at any stage.

'Sticking' points

Some common 'sticking' points for settlement in stroke claims are similar to that of other clinical negligence cases, irrespective of the value, and can include:

- If an order for Provisional Damages is sought. For example, to protect against the risk of epilepsy developing.

- Whether settlement is to be on a lump sum basis or a Periodical Payment Order. (A form of award report may be required (which would not be disclosed to the defendant).)

- Recognising the risks to both parties in the litigation and being prepared to make reasonable compromises to reflect this.

- Appreciating the position of the opponent.

- Inability to obtain instructions on the proposal. For example, if the defendant stipulates that they have reached the limit of their authority to negotiate and cannot do so further without instructions.

- Understandably, the potential stark difference between the parties in the Schedule of Loss and Counter Schedule and expert evidence.

Tackling 'sticking points' can often be fraught with challenges. Revisiting the goals (of the claimant) might assist to reflect upon what are deemed the most important aspects and aspirations regarding a proposed settlement. Some parts could be a 'deal breaker' (seeking Provisional Damages for example) and other components may be up for concessions and compromises. Preparing well for settlement negotiations will support the best prospects of being able to reach a resolution as it is not uncommon to encounter an impasse. Being well-prepared to try and navigate any solutions will help deliver the foremost results.

High value stroke claims in particular demand a scrupulous analysis of all the issues in preparation for settlement considerations. Preparing so called "Scott Schedules" and detailed analysis with multiple variables / permutations of outcomes will give a clearer vision to what could be achieved. It will also assist identifying the obstacles that might arise and how to combat such issues. The amount of work required can be extensive but it is paramount to strenuously prepare for ADR in order to produce the desired outcomes and give the opportunity to overcome a possible stalemate.

ADR Meeting

A face-to-face/video/hybrid meeting between the parties is often necessary to facilitate structured negotiations to try and reach a resolution. Sometimes, liability only meetings can occur. These can be helpful, even when a compromise is not achieved as disputed issues can be narrowed. However, if one party is only making liability offers and the opponent is not engaging in the same process (which is potentially not in itself unreasonable) then this might hinder progress for a possible resolution. For example, a claimant may be eager to settle in full. Consequently, they may decide to only make quantum offers, perhaps factoring liability concessions within such offers, whereas the defendant may not wish to engage in quantum settlement at that juncture for various reasons.

Making the opponent aware in advance of the intentions during a meeting for ADR and continuing any progressive dialogue beforehand can facilitate more constructive discussions surrounding settlement possibilities. The recurring theme of sufficiently preparing in advance is pertinent. Having the ability to negotiate on both liability and quantum can be useful, and a possible strategy, even when it is proposed for a liability only meeting. However, it cannot be expected that both parties will have the same prerogative.

Stroke claims can be likened to brain injury claims in respect of quantum issues for settlement. This text is not an in-depth analysis on quantification issues at an ADR meeting (as a text in itself could be written on that topic) but very broadly, some underlying points to consider in advance of an ADR meeting include:

- Whether to have a pre-ADR conference with the claimant/counsel/experts.

- Managing expectations and preparing the claimant/their family for what could arise in the settlement/ADR process. This can include things such as negotiating on a lump sum basis or for Periodical Payments, along with setting out possible quantum parameters.

- The platform for the meeting. Being in person can be especially productive and the claimant may desire to be face-to-face. Be acutely aware of any communication/fatigue/mobility challenges they may have in order to promote/enable their participation at any ADR meeting.

- Preparing any bundles/submissions/skeleton arguments or similar – for use with the opponents and/or for the claimant/counsel.

- Preparing a forensic assessment of the claim and meticulous instructions to counsel (if counsel is leading the ADR meeting).

During an ADR meeting, ultimately, all heads of loss and items claimed for settlement could be subject to negotiation and there will be occasions when ADR is unsuccessful and further negotiations may occur at a later date/event. Bracing a claimant for this possible outcome (and ADR meetings being postponed) can assist in managing expectations. ADR meetings can be intense for the claimant and hitches can undoubtedly occur. Supporting the claimant prior to and during the process is essential.

Approval hearings and Anonymity Orders

In cases where the claimant is a protected party because they lack capacity to instruct solicitors and manage finances, or they are a child, the approval of court to any interim payments and settlement will be required pursuant to CPR Part 21.10. A significant amount of work can be involved at this stage including obtaining written advice on the proposed settlement, preparing bundles, some of which will be confidential and only for the judge and organising various other matters.

If the claimant is a child or protected party, an anonymity order may be required. However, consideration for seeking such an order should be given at the first stage of proceedings being issued. Whether this be via the Part 7 or Part 8 process. The draft order is available online using the following link (at the time of writing):

https://www.gov.uk/government/publications/form-pf10-anonymity-and-prohibition-of-publication-order

Practitioners should be alive to the recent judgment in *PMC (a child by his mother and litigation friend FLR) v A Local Health Board* [2024] EWHC 2969 (KB) where Nicklin J refused to grant the claimant anonymity or to impose any restrictions on reporting the case. The claimant was a child that had developed cerebral palsy from admitted clinical negligence but the mother/litigation friend had previously engaged in media coverage commenting on the claimant's injuries and difficulties. Permission has been granted to appeal this decision and it will be a point to keep under review. Therefore, if making an application for anonymity:

- The application should be made promptly at the outset of proceedings.

- Provide clear evidence within the application.

- Notice of the application should be sent to any relevant party and in particular, if there has been previous media publishing in the claim.

- Advise the litigation friend early in the matter before they consider engaging in any media (including social media posts) that it could impact the ability to obtain a future anonymity order.

An apology and impact statements

The claimant may invite an apology from the defendant, even if an apology letter has already been provided. Sometimes an apology is given with the Letter of Response. Most claimants are not seeking punishment or retribution but for lessons to be learned and for improvements to be made. Consider in advance whether the claimant is seeking an apology and if so, in what form and whether this is achievable. If an apology is given at a RTM/JSM/Mediation, this is usually at the conclusion of a claim once it is settled.

Similarly, the claimant may wish to provide an impact statement at a resolution/ADR meeting. There should be co-operative dialogue between the parties beforehand so each attendee is aware of the intentions for an impact statement to be read out, and by whom. Once a claim is settled, there can be a range of emotions from the claimant and their family. It is more usual for any impact statements to be read/delivered at the beginning of a meeting. This might assist a claimant or their family to feel their voice/concerns/feedback is being heard and that lessons can be learned.

Fundamental dishonesty (FD)

It may seem incongruous to discuss fundamental dishonesty (FD) within a 'settlement' chapter but claimants should be advised during their case on the FD regime. It appears to be becoming more prevalent in clinical negligence than it has been over the past decade since section 57 Criminal Justice and Courts Act 2015 introduced the new zero tolerance culture for fraud in injury claims. If the court is satisfied on the balance of probabilities that a claimant has been fundamentally dishonest their successful claim to damages can be dismissed.

In *London Organising Committee of the Olympic and Paralympic Games (In Liquidation) v Sinfield* [2018] EWHC 51 (QB) the court set out the approach to applications under the Criminal Justice and Courts Act 2015 to have a personal injury claim dismissed for FD. A claimant should be found to be fundamentally dishonest within the meaning of section 57(1)(b) if:

- The defendant proved on a balance of probabilities that they had acted dishonestly in relation to the primary claim and/or a related claim (as defined in section 57(8)); and

- That it substantially affected the presentation of the case, in respect of either liability or quantum in a way which potentially adversely affected the defendant in a significant way; and

- Judged in the context of the particular facts and circumstances of the litigation.

- If the judge was satisfied, they had to dismiss the claim, including any element of the primary claim in respect of which the claimant had not been dishonest, unless, they were satisfied that the claimant would suffer substantial injustice.

Substantial injustice had to mean more than the mere fact that the claimant would lose their damages for those heads of claim that were not tainted with dishonesty. A recent example of FD being applied in clinical negligence is *Brown v (1) Liverpool University Hospitals NHS Foundation Trust and (2) Mersey and West Lancashire Hospitals NHS Trust* [2024] Med LR 494 whereby the purported claim for loss of earnings was assessed as being dishonest resulting in the primary claim being dismissed. The dishonesty surrounding the inflated loss of earnings claim presented was regarded as going to the heart of the claim and thus, it was fundamentally dishonest.

In determining whether there will be substantial injustice in dismissing the claim, a very high bar is in place with more than the mere loss of damages being required to potentially establish a substantial injustice. In *Wye Valley NHS Trust v Murphy* [2022] EWHC 3386 (KB) the court determined there would not be substantial injustice in dismissing the claim. The Trust had previously admitted negligence and provided interim payments, which the claimant was ordered to repay along with indemnity costs. *Muyepa* (see chapter six) is another example of the court adopting a hard-line approach and dismissing the primary claim.

In *McCabe*, (as outlined in chapter two regarding the use of the GP Oxford Handbook) it is of note that the defendant obtained surveillance evidence on the claimant. Quantum was agreed in the sum of £150,000, despite the claimant initially seeking around £1million. However, this was pleaded on the basis of the claimant deteriorating in future due to a poor prognosis. Interestingly, the defendant abandoned their attack on the claimant's credibility after the claimant gave evidence and the judge, Sir Robert Nelson, stated:

> "*I am entirely satisfied that the Defendants were correct to abandon any attack on the Claimant's credibility… I formed the clear view that they were decent honest people.*"

It is pellucidly clear from this example that in stroke litigation a claimant can be placed under surveillance. Further, they can have their credibility and extent of injuries subject to intense scrutiny and challenge with no repercussions in failing to establish FD.

Calderdale & Huddersfield NHS Trust v Metcalf [2021] EWHC 611 (QB) is an example of a claimant being sentenced to six months imprisonment after a finding of FD for exaggerating her physical disabilities amongst other things. Similarly, in *North Bristol NHS Trust v White* [2022] EWHC 1313 (QB) the claimant was sentenced to six months imprisonment after Ritchie J found the claimant was fundamentally dishonest in matters such as their walking distance, using stairs and the use of walking aids. The prominence of surveillance in clinical negligence appears to be growing.

Shaw v Wilde [2024] EWHC 1660 (KB) is another recent example of the severity of FD being found. This was a road traffic accident personal injury claim that was struck out despite His Honour Judge Sephton KC finding the genuine value of the claim was £1,230,145.60. A stark warning that the courts are not readily finding substantial injustice irrespective of life-changing injuries. Something more than the loss of damages is required for the hurdle of substantial injustice to be overcome in the event of a finding of FD.

In *Cullen v Henniker-Major* [2024] EWHC 2809 the defendants alleged FD and evidenced social media posts along with covert video surveillance but the claimant was not held to be dishonest. Bearing in mind this claimant contended that full-time care was required, it is explicit that defendants will not shy away from investigating and alleging FD, despite significant injuries being sustained. In the context of stroke, there remains the potential that FD could be pleaded in claims of any value if it is deemed by defendants to merit that argument.

The operation of FD is seen as greatly in favour of defendants (by the claimant sector; perhaps not by defendants). It remains to be seen whether any reform or developments occur surrounding claims of unfounded allegations of FD.

Highlights for FD:

- Carefully explain the significance of signing a statement of truth each time one is signed.

- Great care should be given when preparing and drafting witness statements and schedules of loss. A claimant should ensure they are factually accurate and forensic rigour should be applied when preparing them.

- Ensure the claimant's current condition, function and extent of activities of daily living is kept up to date. Any change of circumstances should be noted and expert/witness evidence updated if necessary.

- Similarly, claimants should confirm that expert reports are accurate and in particular, that medical and care/OT reports are up to date and express the correct condition of the claimant before they are disclosed.

- Fundamental does not mean significant. One misleading aspect of a part of the claimant's claim can readily be judged as fundamental.

- In the event that FD is established and the retainer remains in place with the claimant, then strong evidence to argue substantial injustice that is more than just the loss of damages will be required.

- The potential incentive for defendants to plead FD outweighs any sanction for doing so and failing to establish FD. There are currently unlikely to be any penalties to a defendant for unsuccessfully pursuing FD.

- Despite stroke often being a life-changing injury, the FD arena appears to be an increasingly evolving area in clinical negligence. Anticipate more stroke (and other) cases to have FD allegations.

Trial

Most stroke cases will not reach trial. Should a trial be impending, significant time will be required to review and prepare for it. Planning ahead will be crucial. By this juncture, joint statements should be available and performing a thorough analysis of the risks in the case will be vital. The focus of time will be spent on matters such as:

- Preparing and holding a pre-trial conference.
- Preparing and attending a Pre-Trial Review or case management hearing.
- Preparing the case summary, skeleton argument, relevant documents, the trial bundle and other necessary preparations.
- Evaluating the pleadings and any further potential applications, amendments, or issues to address.
- Summonsing witnesses and arranging for their attendance.

There will be a superabundance of work to undertake in the buildup to a trial but the opportunity for settlement remains when preparing for trial, and during trial. It can be useful to arrange a RTM before the trial, even if it is a second, or perhaps even a third RTM. Enabling the process of constructive, ongoing dialogue between the parties will usually maximise the prospects of a settlement being possible without either party having the risk of the 'all or nothing' outcome at trial. Adopting a rigid approach with no flexibility will more likely create obstacles to settlement, rather than demonstrating confidence in the case.

Settlement overview

Dispute resolution is a key process to be engaged in by the parties during a stroke claim. It is not distinct from other clinical negligence claims in this regard. A summary is:

- Outline options to the claimant for their instructions.
- Prepare diligently in advance of any negotiations/ADR/meeting. Detailed and fastidious preparation is imperative.
- Do not underestimate the use of impact statements and an authentic apology.
- Fundamental dishonesty being alleged is becoming ever more present in clinical negligence claims.
- ADR/settlement can occur at many points during the claim. Keep the goal of settlement in mind when progressing cases.

EPILOGUE

As set out in the Introduction to this book, stroke prevalence remains on the rise and it is projected to continually increase. With the limited resources available in the NHS and scarcity of neurologists, stroke physicians, rehabilitation medicine consultants and various other clinicians, it is incontrovertible that much is to be done to help reduce the prominence of stroke and the outcomes following stroke. This is undoubtedly going to be a monumental challenge to the NHS. It is axiomatic that the oft quoted phrase 'prevention is better than cure' (often attributed to the Dutch philosopher Desiderius Erasmus) is relevant here.

It is incumbent that improvements and developments continue, in order to shift the current trend of the proliferating numbers of stroke. Improving healthcare and systems directed at the prevention of stroke is paramount and with there being a strong emphasis on the clinical priority of stroke, it could be anticipated that guidelines and policies will be updated as matters evolve.

Looking ahead to the future, with scientific innovation and more stroke studies being published, it may be, for example, that the effects of thrombolysis can be enhanced and be shown to reduce the impact/effects of stroke to a greater extent. Further studies could go on to demonstrate that a greater proportion of people will have more favourable outcomes long term due to receiving thrombolysis. This could pave the way for developments of liability/causation issues in stroke claims relating to giving thrombolysis.

More importantly however, it could help deliver better outcomes for people following stroke. Issues surrounding causation and material contribution are a dynamic aspect of clinical negligence and stroke claims could feature as part of any potential transformation.

There remains much to be developed in the burgeoning arena of stroke litigation and it is foreseeable that there is more to come.

MORE BOOKS BY LAW BRIEF PUBLISHING

A selection of our other titles available now:-

'A Practical Guide to Probation Breaches and Other Applications' by Mark Thomas
'A Practical Guide to Remarriage and Divorce' by Cordelia Williams & Claire Howard
'A Practical Guide to Privacy, Transparency, Reporting Restrictions and Closed Proceedings in the Court of Protection' by Laura Mannering
'Beaumont on Barristers – A Guide to Defending Disciplinary Proceedings (Second Edition)' by Marc Beaumont
'A Practical Guide to Payments for Environmental Services' by Ben Sharples
'A Practical Guide to the Law of Pregnancy and Maternity at Work' by Rebecca Thomas
'A Practical Guide to Redundancy – Second Edition' by Philip Hyland & Collette Moore
'A Practical Guide to International Issues for Scottish Family Lawyers' by Susie Mountain, Donna McKay, Ken MacDonald
'A Practical Guide to the Law on Deprivation of Liberty' by Ben Troke
'A Practical Guide to Rights over Airspace and Subsoil – Second Edition' by Daniel Gatty
'A Practical Guide to the Law in Relation to Inquests' by Ramya Nagesh
'A Practical Guide to the Construction and Rectification of Wills and Trust Instruments (Second Edition)' by Edward Hewitt
'A Practical Guide to Data Protection in Social Housing' by Clare Paterson
'A Practical Guide to Spousal Maintenance – Second Edition' by Liz Cowell
'A Practical Guide to International Parental Child Abduction Law (England and Wales)' by Dr Onyója Momoh
'A Practical Guide to Deprivation of British Citizenship' by Sean Ell
'A Practical Guide to Commercial Property Service Charges' by Rachel Garton
'A Practical Guide to Clinical Negligence – Third Edition' by Geoffrey Simpson-Scott (Geoff)
'A Practical Guide to the Rights of Grandparents in Children Proceedings – Second Edition' by Stuart Barlow

‘The Electronic Communications Code: A Practical Guide – Second Edition’ by Kerry Bretherton KC, James Castle, Mark Loveday
‘A Practical Guide to the Independent School Standards – September 2023 Edition’ by Sarah McKimm
'A Practical Guide to Estate Administration and Crypto Assets' by Richard Marshall
‘A Practical Guide to Parental Alienation in Private and Public Law Children Cases’ by Sam King QC & Frankie Shama
‘Contested Heritage – Removing Art from Land and Historic Buildings’ by Richard Harwood QC, Catherine Dobson, David Sawtell
‘The Limits of Separate Legal Personality: When Those Running a Company Can Be Held Personally Liable for Losses Caused to Third Parties Outside of the Company’ by Dr Mike Wilkinson
‘A Practical Guide to Transgender Law’ by Robin Moira White & Nicola Newbegin
‘A Practical Guide to ‘Stranded Spouses’ in Family Law’ by Mani Singh Basi
‘A Practical Guide to Residential Freehold Conveyancing’ by Lorraine Richardson
‘A Practical Guide to Pensions on Divorce for Lawyers’ by Bryan Scant
‘A Practical Guide to Challenging Sham Marriage Allegations in Immigration Law’ by Priya Solanki
‘A Practical Guide to Digital Communications Evidence in Criminal Law’ by Sam Willis
‘A Practical Guide to Legal Rights in Scotland’ by Sarah-Jane Macdonald
‘A Practical Guide to New Build Conveyancing’ by Paul Sams & Rebecca East
‘A Practical Guide to Inherited Wealth on Divorce’ by Hayley Trim
‘A Practical Guide to Practice Direction 12J and Domestic Abuse in Private Law Children Proceedings’ by Rebecca Cross & Malvika Jaganmohan
‘A Practical Guide to Confiscation and Restraint’ by Narita Bahra QC, John Carl Townsend, David Winch
‘A Practical Guide to the Law of Forests in Scotland’ by Philip Buchan
‘A Practical Guide to Health and Medical Cases in Immigration Law’ by Rebecca Chapman & Miranda Butler
‘A Practical Guide to Bad Character Evidence for Criminal Practitioners by Aparna Rao
‘A Practical Guide to Extradition Law post-Brexit’ by Myles Grandison et al
‘A Practical Guide to Hoarding and Mental Health for Housing Lawyers’ by Rachel Coyle

'Stephens on Contractual Indemnities' by Richard Stephens
'A Practical Guide to the EU Succession Regulation' by Richard Frimston
'A Practical Guide to Solicitor and Client Costs – Second Edition' by Robin Dunne
'Constructive Dismissal – Practice Pointers and Principles' by Benjimin Burgher
'A Practical Guide to Religion and Belief Discrimination Claims in the Workplace' by Kashif Ali
'A Practical Guide to the Law of Medical Treatment Decisions' by Ben Troke
'Fundamental Dishonesty and QOCS in Personal Injury Proceedings: Law and Practice' by Jake Rowley
'A Practical Guide to the Law in Relation to School Exclusions' by Charlotte Hadfield & Alice de Coverley
'A Practical Guide to Divorce for the Silver Separators' by Karin Walker
'The Right to be Forgotten – The Law and Practical Issues' by Melissa Stock
'A Practical Guide to Planning Law and Rights of Way in National Parks, the Broads and AONBs' by James Maurici QC, James Neill et al
'A Practical Guide to Election Law' by Tom Tabori
'A Practical Guide to the Law in Relation to Surrogacy' by Andrew Powell
'A Practical Guide to Claims Arising from Fatal Accidents – Second Edition' by James Patience
'A Practical Guide to Asbestos Claims' by Jonathan Owen & Gareth McAloon
'A Practical Guide to Stamp Duty Land Tax in England and Northern Ireland' by Suzanne O'Hara
'A Practical Guide to the Law of Farming Partnerships' by Philip Whitcomb
'A Practical Guide to the Law of Unlawful Eviction and Harassment – Second Edition' by Stephanie Lovegrove
'A Practical Guide to Costs in Personal Injury Claims – Second Edition' by Matthew Hoe
'A Practical Guide to the General Data Protection Regulation (GDPR) – Second Edition' by Keith Markham
'A Practical Guide to Working with Litigants in Person and McKenzie Friends in Family Cases' by Stuart Barlow
'Protecting Unregistered Brands: A Practical Guide to the Law of Passing Off' by Lorna Brazell
'A Practical Guide to Secondary Liability and Joint Enterprise Post-Jogee' by Joanne Cecil & James Mehigan

'A Practical Guide to the Pre-Action RTA Claims Protocol for Personal Injury Lawyers' by Antonia Ford
'A Practical Guide to Neighbour Disputes and the Law' by Alexander Walsh
'A Practical Guide to Coercive Control for Legal Practitioners and Victims' by Rachel Horman
'A Practical Guide to the Law of Driverless Cars – Second Edition'
by Alex Glassbrook, Emma Northey & Scarlett Milligan
'A Practical Guide to TOLATA Claims' by Greg Williams
'A Practical Guide to Elderly Law – Second Edition' by Justin Patten
'A Practical Guide to Responding to Housing Disrepair and Unfitness Claims' by Iain Wightwick
'A Practical Guide to the Law of Bullying and Harassment in the Workplace' by Philip Hyland
'How to Be a Freelance Solicitor: A Practical Guide to the SRA-Regulated Freelance Solicitor Model' by Paul Bennett
'A Practical Guide to Prison Injury Claims' by Malcolm Johnson
'A Practical Guide to Advising Clients at the Police Station' by Colin Stephen McKeown-Beaumont
'A Practical Guide to Antisocial Behaviour Injunctions – Second Edition' by Iain Wightwick
'Practical Mediation: A Guide for Mediators, Advocates, Advisers, Lawyers, and Students in Civil, Commercial, Business, Property, Workplace, and Employment Cases' by Jonathan Dingle with John Sephton
'The Mini-Pupillage Workbook' by David Boyle
'A Practical Guide to Crofting Law' by Brian Inkster
'A Practical Guide to the Law of Domain Names and Cybersquatting' by Andrew Clemson
'A Practical Guide to the Law of Gender Pay Gap Reporting' by Harini Iyengar
'NHS Whistleblowing and the Law' by Joseph England
'Employment Law and the Gig Economy' by Nigel Mackay & Annie Powell
'A Practical Guide to Noise Induced Hearing Loss (NIHL) Claims' by Andrew Mckie, Ian Skeate, Gareth McAloon
'An Introduction to Beauty Negligence Claims – A Practical Guide for the Personal Injury Practitioner' by Greg Almond
'Intercompany Agreements for Transfer Pricing Compliance' by Paul Sutton
'Zen and the Art of Mediation' by Martin Plowman
'A Practical Guide to Adoption for Family Lawyers' by Graham Pegg

www.ingramcontent.com/pod-product-compliance
Ingram Content Group UK Ltd.
Pitfield, Milton Keynes, MK11 3LW, UK
UKHW021238300926
15471UKWH00013B/665

9 781916 698871